Why Not?

Why Not?

The Art of Ginny Ruffner

Bonnie J. Miller

Introduction by Arthur C. Danto

A Samuel and Althea Stroum Book

Tacoma Art Museum in association with the
University of Washington Press • Seattle & London

To my husband, Ed, whose love, generosity, and support enrich my life. —B.J.M.

This book is published with the assistance of a grant from the Stroum Book Fund,
established through the generosity of Samuel and Althea Stroum.

Why Not? The Art of Ginny Ruffner is published concurrently with the exhibition *Gardens of Delight,*
curated by Barbara Johns and organized by the Tacoma Art Museum, Tacoma, Washington,
December 15, 1995–March 24, 1996.

Designers: Katy Homans and Deborah Zeidenberg
Editors: Lorna Price and Patricia Draher
Publication Coordinator: Mary Clure

All photographs by Michael Seidl except: pp. 17–20: Bard Wrisley; pp. 40–41: Robert Lyons; p. 45: Nicholas Williams;
pp. 53–55: Joel Breger; p. 56: Paul Warchol; pp. 86–87: Alan McCoy; pp. 73 and 99: photographer unknown

Library of Congress Cataloging-in-Publication Data
Miller, Bonnie J.
    Why Not?: The Art of Ginny Ruffner / Bonnie J. Miller.
      p. cm.
    "A Samuel and Althea Stroum book."
    "Published concurrently with the exhibition Gardens of Delight, curated by Barbara Johns and organized by the
Tacoma Art Museum, Tacoma, Washington, December 15, 1995–March 24, 1996"—T.p. verso.
    ISBN 0-295-97508-3
    1. Ruffner, Ginny—Criticism and interpretation. I. Ruffner, Ginny. II. Miller, Bonnie J. III. Tacoma Art Museum. IV. Title.
NK5198.R83M55 1995
730'.92—dc20
                                    95-36629
                                    CIP

Front cover: *Balance Series/Theory of Applied Decoration,* 1995, lampworked glass and mixed media, 18 x 15 x 6 in.

Back cover: *La Donna Mobile,* 1990, lampworked glass and mixed media, 24 x 21 x 15 in.

Frontispiece: *Pondering Women–Yellow Feather,* 1991, lampworked glass and mixed media, 18 x 29 x 14 in.

Printed and bound in Hong Kong

Contents

Acknowledgments

In her book *Writing Down the Bones*, Natalie Goldberg quotes Zen master Dainin Katagiri Roshi on success: "Your little will can't do anything. It takes Great Determination. Great Determination doesn't mean just you making an effort. It means the whole universe is behind you and with you—the birds, trees, sky, moon, and ten directions." This book is the result of great determination in the form of many people's efforts.

I thank Barbara Johns and Chase W. Rynd of the Tacoma Art Museum for their belief in the book and the Museum for agreeing to take on the project.

Samuel and Althea Stroum generously supported this publication. Donald R. Ellegood, Naomi B. Pascal, Pat Soden, and others at the University of Washington Press offered much encouragement. The Linda Farris Gallery, Seattle; Fay Gold Gallery, Atlanta; Habatat Galleries, Pontiac and Boca Raton; Heller Gallery, New York; Maurine Littleton Gallery, Washington, D.C.; Meyerson and Nowinski Art Associates, Seattle; Betsy Rosenfield Gallery, Chicago; and Jeffrey Rhodes have all contributed to making this book a reality.

I appreciate Arthur C. Danto's eloquent introduction and Chase W. Rynd's inspiring remarks for this book. I thank Mary Clure, who coordinated the many details of the publication project, Lorna Price for her keen editorial knowledge and guidance, Patricia Draher for copy editing, and Katy Homans, whose imaginative design skills brought the book to life.

Ginny Ruffner patiently participated in hours and hours of interviews, and saw possibilities and hope even when the project's outcome seemed uncertain. Her staff, especially Jeff Simmons and Julie Haack, were always willing to help find photos, look something up, or distract the cat.

I especially thank my supporter, Claudia Finseth, without whose help this manuscript would never have found its way, as well as Kay Pullen for her invaluable input, and Deanna Dally for listening over countless cups of tea.

Finally, my family's love and encouragement sustained me throughout the writing. For their support I thank my husband, Ed, my children, Lila and Zach, my mother, Eleanor Balzer, and my sister, Ann Lawrence.

—B.J.M.

Foreword

Many years ago I was introduced to Ginny Ruffner at an art auction and was immediately drawn into the constellation of her admirers. My status of fan soon evolved into that of friend. I later discovered that Ginny has an uncanny capacity to absorb many new friends into her life while at the same time maintaining strong and consistent bonds with her old ones. Being a friend of Ginny Ruffner is to be in very good company. It is also a place of honor, since she makes each of us feel that we are the most important person in her life. She gives—to her friends and to the world as a whole—much more than could ever be returned. It was, therefore, with both humility and joy that I readily agreed to write this foreword. In this brief attempt to convey how greatly she has affected our community, I hope she will recognize the underlying message of respect and gratitude that we have for her and her work.

To know Ginny Ruffner is to be perpetually astonished by her. Outstanding among her many attributes are her incisive wit, her disciplined intellect, and her balanced sense of aesthetics—all continually demonstrated in her work. She is also a woman of tremendous courage who lives (and broadcasts) her convictions. Most important, she supports her community and passionately believes in the role of art as a social imperative. Several years ago Ginny brought her considerable skills to Tacoma. Engaged as a guest curator, she conceived the exhibition *Glass: Material in the Service of Meaning*. This was a critically important show for our region, as it simultaneously focused on glass as the central medium and emphasized the secondary nature of that medium when viewed in the context of the purpose of art. She clearly indicated that glass, in all of its artistic manifestations, is first and foremost a vehicle utilized by the artist as a mode of expression. Content, shaped by experience, perspective, and contemplation, is the ultimate force behind a successful creative work, and glass is simply one of the raw materials the artist forges to convey that content.

The Tacoma Art Museum has reaffirmed its commitment to art and artists of the Pacific Northwest. Given the status of glass in our region, enhanced by the presence of the extraordinary Pilchuck Glass School, it is only natural that we regularly exhibit and collect local artists who work in glass. An exhibition scheduled for the winter of 1995–96, *Gardens of Delight*, includes glass by Ginny Ruffner and several other well-known artists. The premise of Ruffner's earlier show remains intact, however, with the content of the work being the driving force.

Ginny Ruffner has had a close association with the Tacoma Art Museum over the past few years. We are very pleased to produce this book to document and celebrate her work. It is a timely and well-deserved effort.

Chase W. Rynd
Executive Director
Tacoma Art Museum

Introduction
Glassy Essences

Arthur C. Danto

But man, proud man,
Drest in a little brief authority,
Most ignorant of
what he's most assured,
His glassy essence . . .
—Shakespeare, *Measure*
for Measure II, ii, 114

I first began to have serious thoughts about Ginny Ruffner's art on the occasion of the opening of her exhibition at the Heller Gallery in New York in early September 1993. The handsome announcement had arrived some weeks before, with an image on its face of a work one could not easily imagine having been done by any artist other than she. Its most salient feature was a circle of mostly face cards—queen and king of clubs, jack of diamonds, a ten of hearts—forming a ring of perhaps ten cards in all, a "hand" dealt in a game whose identity I could not make out. From within this hand, an arrangement of hands—human hands, this time, their palms displayed—reaches up toward what seems to be a golden ring. The ring is but the topmost link in a chain of rings, the lowest link of which is fastened to an ascending zigzag form in blue, like a ladder or a trellis, which culminates in a valentine-style heart. Several more hearts appear in the work: on the ten of hearts, at the top of the blue zigzag, like an espaliered heart tree. Hearts are carried by two plump, flesh-pink, doll-like figures climbing down the zigzag as if they had been engaged in a harvesting of hearts. Finally, each of the ascending hands has a single eye staring out of its palm, as in some ancient symbolism. One has seen the eye-in-palm symbol, perhaps in some Tantric work, where eyes are given odd loci across the body, or possibly in an advertisement for the Gypsy fortune teller who will, by turning cards, disclose the secret knowledge for which we thirst. What fortune teller—reader of cards, or reader of palms—will deliver to us the meaning of this complex glass montage? It was in any case a work I wanted to see.

The title of the work is *The Secrets of Eye Hand Coordination* (p. 82), and it is one of two pieces by Ginny Ruffner, both made in 1993, that are illustrated on the invitation. The second work, like this one, could have been the artistic invention of no other artist. Ginny Ruffner's work is unmistakably hers, even if no two of her works look exactly alike, and having seen only one of her pieces, one will be able to recognize anything she does as hers, instantly and intuitively, even if one cannot easily answer the question of what, beyond "a Ruffner," the work is, or what it means. Somehow, one feels, the "secret" must have to do with the heart—perhaps with "taking heart," like the little descending harvesters who, as in a charade, may be enacting the phrase for taking courage.

The second work is titled *What's Really in the Space between Integers?* (p. 88). The work displays the answer, like a prompt-card, in case the viewer should falter: it is the infinity sign, which Ruffner has formed, rather comically, as if it were squeezed out of a tube, or as if someone were obliged to make the austere symbol out of a closed loop of sausages. The remainder of the montage is made up of drawings by Paul Klee, and then a number of highly ornamental bands and ribbonlike forms, twisted loosely together with the infinity sign and the recognizable Klees—the *Twittering Machine* and the wry *Bavarian Don Giovanni*, in which a stick figure, wearing a Tyrolian hat, climbs a ladder through a space with the names of Bavarian girls as constellations. The Spanish Don Giovanni had Doña Elvira, Doña Anna, Zerbinetta; his Bavarian counterpart has Emma, Mari, Kathi, Cenzl, and Theres. In Spain there were "one thousand and three" seductees. How many in Bavaria? Answer: "What's really in the space between integers?" So, an infinite number of conquests! The work is less mathematical than erotic, and more playful than it is either. I have no idea of why Klee's *Isola Dulcimara* of 1938 is in the work, or why a particularly realistic tiger lily is thrust into the montage like a rose into the coiffeur of a Spanish flirt. But my overall sense is that the conjunction of three images by Paul Klee, with no internal relationship between them, is a warning not to press for a more systematic interpretation than we have. The work has an "answer"—it *is* an answer, since its title is a question. But it does not hold a secret, except that there is doubtless more to the work than the answer to that question.

I have used the word "montage" in rather a promiscuous way to characterize these two pieces by Ginny Ruffner, mindful that standardly the term has been used in connection with cinema, and with a certain cut-and-paste way of dealing with photographic images, which was invented by Berlin dada in the early 1920s or possibly earlier.

The classical photomontage—if "classical" can be used without irony for an art form so rowdy and subversive—consisted of two or more heterogeneous components from different photographic sources, fitted together to create a new meaning by juxtaposition. It is sometimes objected that these should be called "collages," but the term was, after all, given by the form's inventors, and it derives from the German verb *montieren,* "to arrange," "assemble," or "fit together." *Monteur* is a German term for "mechanic," and it was almost certainly the proletarian connotations the term evoked that appealed to the radicals in the dada movement, who liked to think of themselves as *Monteuren* rather than artists.

Montage carries its meaning over into cuisine: a *salade montée* is the precise opposite of a tossed salad—and if a salad maker were to get carried away by the connotations and compose a salad consisting of fish, meat, and fowl—hence water, earth, and air, so that the dish is a small allegory of the cosmos—he would have achieved a mannerist work in the medium of edibility. The term "assemblage" has of course long been used to identify a form of sculpture composed of disparate parts and pieces, but in extending the term montage to cover Ruffner's glass sculpture, we mark a spirit it may share with dada photomontage, and may in addition signal a kind of sorority between Ruffner and the great dada *Monteur* Hannah Hoch, who also used dolls and doll-like effigies to expressive purpose. Montage thus emphasizes the kind of sculptures Ruffner makes, and helps dissolve some of the resistance that their medium, glass, sets up to thinking of their continuities to other forms of art. For all the solidarity between Ruffner and her fellow artists in glass, it is of some value to think of her as a *Monteur* who happens to use glass, rather than a glass artist whose closest aesthetic kin will be found among other glass artists. The fact that lampwork requires a technical skill in the handling of the material deepens the connection between her work and the politics of montage in Berlin dada.

These two montages, in any case, typified the work she exhibited at the Heller Gallery in September 1993, but they typify as well the entirety of Ruffner's artistic production as far back as it is perhaps relevant to trace it. Characteristically, though not invariably, these works have a kind of carousel form, a closed circle in which repeated objects are arranged in a ring, like the pencils in the second tier of the cakelike *The Power of Words to Invent Beauty* of 1990, or the miniature versions of famous paintings of women's faces—by Botticelli, Picasso, Matisse, Leonardo, Kahlo, etc.—affixed to glass bodies ranged like Rockettes holding hands, in *Beauty Deconstructing Portraiture* of the same year (or like the playing cards in *The Secrets of Eye Hand Coordination* of 1993). Ruffner's works are further marked by fond art historical references, by a spirit of comedy, by a certain sassy intellectualism in the titles (deconstruction and integers, for example, are terms available only to someone who has done a certain amount of reading in relatively abstruse texts), and by a kind of preoccupation with the puzzles and problems of aesthetic perception. These concerns were seasoned by deeper and more personal meanings in the work of 1993 and the work since, to which I will return. For the moment, though, I want to go back to my remembered impressions of Ruffner's opening that evening at the Heller Gallery.

I remember walking among these extravagant inventions, dense with intelligence and dark with comedy, each presumably the embodiment of a thesis or an allegory or at the very least a riddle, and collectively implying an audience prepared to respond to the artistic and intellectual challenge to open up the works' secrets or solve the riddles they propounded or to catch the joke or pun at the work's heart. The work implied an audience of a singular refinement, and it paid in consequence an extreme compliment to those who came to view it. I thought all at once that the closest artistic peer these intricate and allusive objects might have in the history of art was Cellini's great salt dish, executed for François I at the court of Fontainebleau around 1540, a work so disproportionate in its symbolic solemnity and power to the simple function it was designed to discharge that it transformed the mere taking of salt into a cosmic ritual if enacted by a king.

A work such as Cellini's implied an audience prepared to appreciate the elaborate references and visual puns, the classical learning and the philosophical vision, the mysterious sympathies between natural forces and their artistic representations, the promise of hidden truths and the pleasures of unconcealing them, that defines the audience Ruffner invents for herself, a very different audience, I think, from the world of glass art with its criteria of appreciation. From the beginning of our acquaintance, I was impressed with the intensity of Ruffner's intellectual ambition, and by her effort to raise the level of discourse of the glass artist. She invited me to address an annual meeting of the Glass Art Society when she served as its president in 1990, and reassured me, when I protested that glass was something, as a philosopher, I knew too little about to feel confident in presenting a talk on any of its aspects before so expert an audience, that what they wanted was some expansion of the horizons within which glass art was practiced. And that, in general, is what she has sought consistently to achieve in her own work, to raise the level of the audience to the level that I suppose had been occupied by the court at Fontainebleau, informed and cunning, and subtle enough to see the whole world in a dish designed to confer a suitable dignity on salt from the sea's substance, and pepper carried unbelievable distances over the sea's surface to lend piquancy to the court's taste.

Perhaps it was the sight of Ginny Ruffner, seated in a wheelchair that night at Heller's, receiving the tribute of her admirers, that evoked the thought of a court in my mind—reinforced, perhaps, by the queen and king of clubs in *The Secrets of Eye Hand Coordination*. The true spice of the evening and of the work was the knowledge that she was exhibiting for the first time since the terrible automobile crash of December 22, 1991, that put her into a coma from which her friends and legions of admirers feared she would not emerge. That event imposed on her an arduous regimen of rehabilitative therapy if she was to have a minimally independent life, let alone an artistically creative one. The show was a triumph of courage and determination, and the quantity of the objects, together with their individual involuted brilliance, was a statement to the world that Ruffner was back, as good an artist as ever, her spirit intact and her saving humor undiminished, even if her smashed self had some distance to traverse before the old hand-eye coordination could be taken for granted and be counted on. Part of that complex work is about reconnecting the damaged circuits between hand and eye, which requires heart. And part of the entire show has to have been about the coordination of hand and eye that defines the kind of art the works exemplify.

The Balance Series is a recent example of the delicate balance between comedy and pathos. In *Balance Series/The Original Checker Cab* of 1994, a checkered monster (p. 90)—and what better metaphor than the regular alternation of black and white to characterize the two sides of the monster's being?—executes a balancing act of body and spirit, emblematized by an artist's palette and a bone, on which its two front paws respectively rest. A clown, wearing the diamond pattern of Harlequin, balances on the checkered back of the beast; a fish atop the clown's head balances on its tail while balancing a glass ewer on its slippery nose. It is a very funny piece, with a funny title, and the clown's whole achievement seems affectingly frivolous—until we realize, as Ginny Ruffner wrote to me, in the capital letters she now uses, that the Balance Series is "ABOUT LEARNING TO WALK AGAIN (IT SURE MAKES ART-MAKING LOOK EASY)." But it would not be consistent with the tremendous ambition of Ruffner's artistic purpose simply to transform into comedy and fun the agony of learning to balance a recalcitrant body in the act of ambulation that most of us have taken for granted since we first learned how to do it. She sees balance as a deeper, more philosophical matter even than this, and wrote, again in her capital letters, "ALSO ABOUT ALL OTHER FORMS OF BALANCE, I E BODY/SOUL, PHYSICAL/MENTAL, LIFE/ART—YOU KNOW—THE EASY STUFF. . . ."

More and more one gets the sense that whatever else they are, Ginny Ruffner's montages are transcripts of her evolving reflections on LIFE/ART, a running commentary on what happens to have been on her eager mind, edifying discourses in glass—confessional, pedagogical, exhortatory, occasionally confrontational but never overbearing, and always luminous with good will. I think glass recommends itself to her for its beauty, but also for the way she can transform it into analyses and interrogations of the concept of beauty which the glass itself exemplifies, so that it becomes self-reflective in a way that mind and language are, and can be gotten to express truths about the "glassy essence" it shares, according to Shakespeare, with us.

In the Beauty Series of 1990–91, Beauty was personified—a "HEADLESS, ARMLESS, WINGED FIGURE THAT HAD ADVENTURES THROUGH VARIOUS ART HISTORICAL/REFERENTIAL SETTINGS," she wrote me in a gloss affixed to a sheet of slides. "I CONTINUE TO EXPLORE THE MEANINGS AND USES OF BEAUTY IN MY WORK—BUT WITHOUT MY LITTLE ALTER-EGO FIGURE." The beauty of the Winged Victory—the aesthetic miracle of that ruined and celebrated figure of the early second century B.C.—is that it has become an almost universal emblem of beauty despite its headless, armless condition. Beauty shines through the wreck and the ruin. For someone who has been through what Ruffner has endured, headlessness and armlessness become conditions not easily sublated by philosophical sublimity. Small wonder the little alter-ego figure has been retired. The title of the Heller exhibition, printed on its announcement, was *When Consciousness Sleeps (Where Does It Go?)*— a Cartesian question into which having undergone coma has been transfigured, as the pain of regaining bodily coordination was transfigured into the symbolic comedy of *The Secrets of Eye Hand Coordination*. My conjecture is that when the body is fully together again, headlessness and armlessness can again possess the luxury of symbolic representations rather than be physiological realities like coma and paralysis. At that time, the little alter ego will make her reappearance, and continue her adventures. Meanwhile, she has left the self-interrogations of beauty behind as a talisman.

Why Not?
The Art of Ginny Ruffner

Bonnie J. Miller

I met Ginny Ruffner for the first time in 1988. An arching vine of glass fruit and flowers topped by an insouciant snake sat on the pedestal before me in the Traver Sutton Gallery in Seattle. Parked within the bower was a glass pickup truck painted gray-blue. The title card read, "My Pickup Truck in the Garden of Eden." This was my second visit to the show that intrigued the eye and mind while tickling the funny bone with such pieces as *The Goddess of the Neon Tetras Shows Off Her New Shoes, If Bananas Ruled the World,* and *Architecture Frying in Succotash Hell.*

I couldn't imagine what the artist would be like who could think up such images and titles. Then suddenly she was standing there, her every-which-way blonde curls making her look taller than she was. Her laugh punctuated a Southern drawl, her clothes were a layering swirl of scarves and jewelry above red cowboy boots. "Is this your truck?" I asked.

"Yep, it is."

"Then you must be Ginny Ruffner," I replied and introduced myself. She took me around the room and told me about the pieces. "Why mermaids and shoes?" I queried.

"Why not?" she laughed. "That's one of the joys of being an artist; you can make anything be possible."

I looked again at the red boots. "I like those."

"Oh, these were a celebration item. I always buy shoes when I have something to celebrate. When the NEA called and told me about my grant, I was out the door and at the store by ten with my credit card in hand." I didn't understand until a long time later that celebrating is not just something Ruffner does on special occasions; celebration is a philosophy of life for her, a daily choice, and one of the basic tenets of her work.

Ginny Ruffner is famous for her lampworked sculpture. But Ruffner is multifaceted, like the gemstone that recurs in her work as a metaphor for opulence, decoration, mystery. If we focus on only one facet of her work at a time, the connections among them are not always clear. But all these facets—glass sculpture, two-dimensional painting, large sculpture, public art, and collaborative work—are cut out of a single stone. Like a diamond, Ruffner's art catches the world and throws it back transformed by her creative genius and perpetual curiosity. Humor dances with Serious Inquiry. Beauty charms Science. Exuberance invites Art History to debate.

Ruffner's art is shaped in part by orientations established in her childhood. Her visual emphasis, her love of narration, her references to literature, and her belief in charm tempered by a well-honed sense of the absurd—all have their roots in her upbringing.

𝒢inny 𝑅uffner 𝑤as 𝑏orn to Al and Carolyn Martin in 1952 in Atlanta, Georgia. Her early years were spent in Trenton, Michigan, where her father, an FBI agent, was assigned. Ruffner was precocious and gained an early command of language. Carolyn Martin also recalls that Ruffner was initially ambidextrous and would draw and write first with one hand, then the other, doing the left side of the page with her left hand and then finishing the right side with the right. This proved efficient for drawing but eventually became confusing because it produced mirror-writing. Ruffner finally learned to write with her left hand only, but she continued to use both hands whenever she painted, even as an adult, doing detail work with the left, background with the right.

Trenton was small and the school had no art program, but Ruffner remembers her first assigned drawing in kindergarten: "We were told to draw something useful. I came home with this white scribbling to show my mother. She said, 'What is it?' and I told her, 'A toilet paper factory.'" She also remembers a field trip in grade school to Greenfield Village, where she saw lampworking for the first time and was "very impressed."

In the summers, the family drove back to Georgia to see relatives, among them Ruffner's maternal grandmother. She was a favorite of Ruffner's because, among other things, she always fixed the child's favorite foods and allowed her to explore her jewelry box, a treasure trove of shiny glitter. The trip, though, was hard on Ruffner, who was prone to car sickness. To distract herself from nausea, she would lie in the back of the family station wagon, watching the scenery flash by, picking out all green or all yellow to focus on, or letting telephone wires and birds come forward, then obliterating them in favor of the background. She called it "tuning her eyes."

Despite these forays into the visual, Ruffner thought she most wanted to be a librarian because, she reasoned, if you were the librarian, you could read all the books. She recounts:

My mother worried because I was such a bookworm. But in retrospect, I attribute all my knowledge to reading. For instance, I have a big vocabulary because I read a lot. I think reading was what fostered my imagination because with books, you have to imagine how things look, how they sound, and how they smell. Books are a true vehicle for the imagination. They can transport you anywhere.

So influenced by words was Ruffner that even now she primarily writes in her sketchbook rather than drawing in it: "If it's drawn, then it's too specific. If it's verbal, then I can make it up in my head. . . . I can imagine how things look, even the notes to myself." Her reading took her everywhere, from the work of the French poet Rimbaud to South American fantasists such as Gabriel García Márquez; from Joseph Campbell and Carl Jung to Stephen Hawking and Jean Baudrillard, feeding her insatiable curiosity and producing a peppering of literary and philosophical references for her sculpture.

Ruffner also attributes her attraction to the narrative mode to the Southern cultural emphasis on the oral tradition and the appreciation of the spoken word:

The narrative tradition is still revered in the South. They have conversations—long, involved, in-depth conversation—and I value that. When I was a child we were not allowed to watch TV during dinner. We had to sit and talk to one another. I think that is good. It forced us to interact and to carry on a conversation, which many times included an element of narration, if only to explain what you did that day.

Perhaps it was also around the dinner table that Ruffner honed her outrageous sense of humor, a quality that helped carry her through the "absurd" Southern tradition of being polite at all costs. In fact, the necessity of being a "steel magnolia" drove her from the South: "If you had ever been to the South, you would know why a smart-aleck female had to leave."

By high school, Ruffner had decided she wanted to be an artist. Her family had moved to Fort Mill, South Carolina, and she took Saturday art classes at the Mint Museum in nearby Charlotte. Her enthusiasm for painting and drawing spilled over to include her friends in the summer of 1970. She taught them to paint, setting them to work copying the irises in her mother's garden. When she told her mother she wanted to make art her career, however, she was met with dismay: "I believed she had such a good mind she could do any number of things, but I thought being an artist was so hard," exclaims Mrs. Martin. "I urged her to do something else and keep art for an avocation." But Ruffner, determined, enrolled in art at Furman College in Greenville, South Carolina, in the fall of 1971. Ruffner recalls:

> I didn't realize that you couldn't just be an art major but that you had to choose a particular type of art. I was thinking about what I liked to do, and I realized that many of the majors, such as printmaking or ceramics, had these elaborate processes. With painting, it was very immediate. The results were right there. Also, I was drawn to painting because of my curiosity about the visible—how we construct it, how we perceive it, and how we communicate it. Painting allowed me to go on to the next step of analysis: after looking at something to see it, you must analyze what you see in order to translate it from your mind to someone else's eyes and mind via the hand.

Ruffner completed her Bachelor of Fine Arts degree in 1974 and her Master of Fine Arts in painting and drawing in 1975 at the University of Georgia in Athens, graduating cum laude and summa cum laude respectively. But the college event that made the greatest impact on her was not sculpture class or painting class but seeing a photo of Marcel Duchamp's famous and enigmatic painting on glass, *The Bride Stripped Bare by Her Bachelors, Even (The Large Glass)* (1915–23).

Duchamp, a French artist who for many years worked in the United States, helped father the dada movement of about 1915 to the mid-1920s as well as the conceptual art movement of the 1960s.[1] With his ready-made objects, among them a urinal and a bird cage filled with marble blocks, he violated the expectation that art must be something physically created by the artist. Instead, he claimed it was choice that defined the artist: choice of object, of form, of combination.[2] He experimented with painting on glass and attached long titles that played on spelling, double entendres, sounds, and meanings. In *The Large Glass*, mechanistic paintings representing the bride and bachelors on separate glass plates were mounted between glass panels in a frame. The enigmatic imagery included a drawing of a chocolate grinder, a water-driven mill wheel, nine "malic moulds," and dust that had accrued on the piece in Duchamp's studio.

Duchamp made other works on glass: *Glider Containing a Water Mill in Neighboring Metals* (1913–15), and *To Be Looked at (from the Other Side of the Glass) with One Eye, Close To, for Almost an Hour* (1918). Duchamp's use of glass and his belief that titles did not just label the works but interacted with them as part of the work were ideas that came like lost relatives to Ruffner's philosophical house.

Though Ruffner doesn't share the dark irony or derision of the dadaists, she likes to play with ideas and language, forming associations that startle us, to express the absurd with a grand cosmic joke—or lots of small puns. A student in the 1970s, Ruffner was midway aesthetically between the elite orientation of late modernism and the inclusive multiplicity of postmodernism. Duchamp seemed to subsume that duality, offering a confluence of head, heart, and humor. Duchamp's influence on Ruffner's work expanded in widening circles as she broke from the modernist and fine art dictums of abstraction and canvas to embrace narrative and glass.

"I realized," says Ruffner, "that glass could add a layer of meaning to anything that it was used for in art because of its historical significance, its fragility, and its controllable transparency." For her master's thesis show, Ruffner painted a series of rectangles on sheets of window glass. Stacked one in front of another, the panes created true rather than illusional three-dimensional space. The layered colors, blending and transmitting through the glass, formed secondary and tertiary hues where they overlapped. Later, Ruffner achieved even more layering of color, experimenting with combinations of oil paint, acrylic paint, colored pencil, cold enamels, graphic marker dye, water color, and pastels: "There are layers and layers of imagery, and layers and layers of paint, and I hope layers of meaning." But color remained secondary in Ruffner's glass work for nearly ten years while she concentrated on form and looked for ways to keep two vows she made when she graduated.

"When I got out of school in 1975, I made a promise to myself to always have a studio because I was familiar enough with motivation to know that a studio, if it is not used, will make you feel guilty, and that makes you work. . . . I also decided to always have a job that required my artistic ability and creativity." The first job, making posters for an advertising agency, quickly led to the second, running a small stained-glass company with a friend from the advertising agency. Ruffner also taught for a short time at a nearby community college. But while she liked teaching art history and water-color painting, she disliked the politics outside the classroom and decided academia was not for her. She found a new direction in an unlikely place:

> One day I went into this glass shop in Atlanta that had all this kitsch, little animals and figurines everywhere. It was awful. But I looked at it and thought, "Think of the possibilities!" I was very excited.
>
> So I called up the shop and asked about a job opening. They didn't hire people without experience but gave me the name of a competitor. The director there said, "Can you engrave glass?" I said, "Sure," believing I could learn to do anything. I bought a diamond engraving tool and a vase and drew a picture on the side of it. I took it to him and he said, "Fine, you are hired," and showed me to this room with all this engraving equipment. I asked, "Could I have a moment alone?" I needed to figure out all the equipment! It wasn't hard, just like drawing. For a year I worked as an engraver, then they let me be an apprentice lampworker. A year later, I called the original shop and said, "I have experience now." I went to work for them, a classical European apprenticeship. I had to do the same thing over and over again, always making it exactly the same. It was good training.

In lampworking, glass rods are heated over a gas torch or burner. Shapes are formed in the glass through manipulation, the use of tools, addition of more glass, and by blowing air into the heated glass through a tube. As her interest and expertise grew, Ruffner used any spare money she had to acquire the necessary tools and supplies to do the lampwork in her own studio. Ruffner's earliest lampworked glass directly relates to standard forms, mostly goblets with stems made of such things as dragonflies and crocodiles. But there are also vegetables—radishes and carrots—two basics of what would become Ruffner's personal iconography:

They are these great subconscious vegetables. If I had a garden, that's what I'd grow—carrots, radishes, and potatoes because they are such beautiful colors and because they are such surprises when you pull them up. It's like fishing and catching something from that whole other world under the water. It's like your subconscious: you don't really know what's there. The ideas surprise you when you pull them out.

As Ruffner's skills expanded, she experimented with new forms, letting her art background come into three-dimensional play.

When we look now at her Dancing Box Series, which began in 1981, it is tempting to see the works only as blank canvases, the fields that in time became filled with everything from tornadoes and paintbrushes to winged beauties and snake goddesses. First, however, Ruffner had to find a form that would not only express her ideas but also deal with the physics of glass sculpture and the limitations of lampworking.

When I first interviewed Ruffner in 1988, I asked her to discuss the biggest problem she found in using glass as a medium: "It breaks," she quipped.

Actually, the glass isn't fragile. In its perfect state, it's stronger than steel. I use borosilicate rods that were developed to be used in the laboratory and are acid, shock, and heat resistant. Borosilicate can be reheated, so when you are doing a lot of work and it cracks, you can do it over. The harder part is figuring out how to get everything in there and still have it balance, have it stand up and not rock.

The Dancing Box Series was sandblasted white as birches, and the forms balanced on three or four pointed legs that resembled sharpened poles in a hunters' camp with skins stretched between them to cure in the sun. According to Ruffner, the pieces were about containment and sensuality. But they also provided commentary on the argument between craft and art concerning the issue of function. As time went on, these forms became more bristled and menacing, belying the gaiety of their "dancer" titles. Though "pristine and boxlike" and requiring "a Pedestal (capital P) and quiet intellectual contemplation,"[3] the series began to take on a more gestural quality as it progressed. *Dancing Box 11* (1983, p. 18) nearly jitterbugs across the floor, and the High Museum piece (1985, p. 19) has lyrical lines that seem too soft to offer even the suggestion of a box.

Even before Ruffner moved from more traditional lampworked forms to sculpture, she was starting to receive recognition in the glass world. One of her vegetable goblets was part of the Leigh Yawkey Woodson Art Museum exhibition *Americans in Glass 1981* in Wausau, Wisconsin. By 1984 she was chosen again for this survey exhibition and for another at Heller Gallery in New York. Her early work culminated in 1985 with a solo show and installation of glass sculpture, *Seven Stations of Intimacy* (p. 20), at Fay Gold Gallery, Atlanta.

This show included large, mixed-media sculpture as well as a grouping of Ruffner's Dancing Boxes. The show comprised one of the earliest illustrations of Ruffner's ability to work in many modes—from small to large scale, from sandblasted lampwork to painted, wall-hung sheet glass. Mixed-media pieces intermingled concrete, neon, even fabric, with plate glass. The exhibition, however, did not reveal changes in Ruffner's personal life that caused such major shifts that they essentially marked a close to the first period of her work and the opening of a second, in which she established the style of glass sculpture that became her signature.

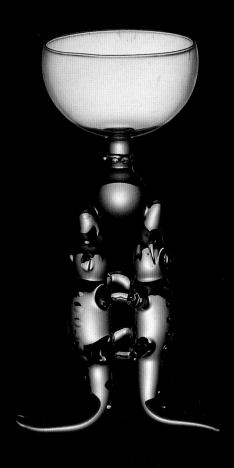

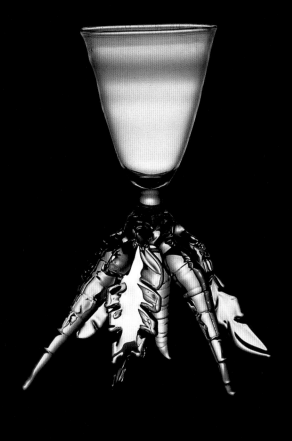

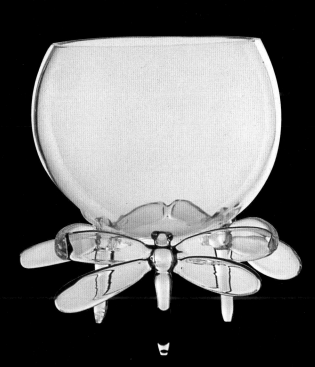

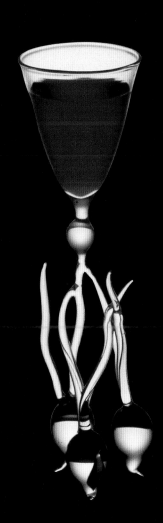

Crocodile Chalice, 1981
Lampworked glass, 8 x 4 x 4 in.

Carrot Cup, 1981
Lampworked glass, 8 x 4 x 4 in.

Dragonfly Bowl, 1981
Lampworked glass, 6 x 6 x 6 in.

Radish Goblet 1, 1981
Lampworked glass, 9 ½ x 2 ½ x 2 ½ in.

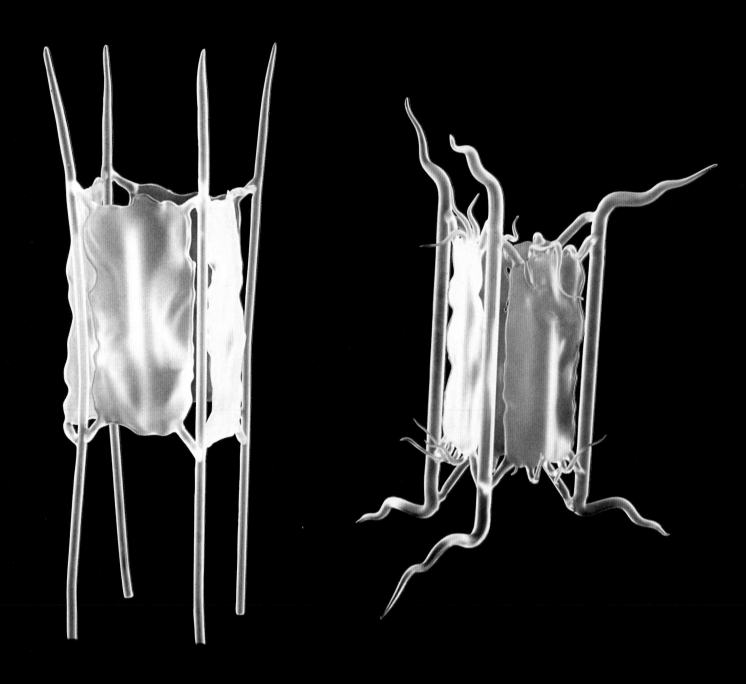

Dancing Box 2, 1983
Sandblasted and lampworked
glass, 30 x 9 x 9 in.

Dancing Box 11, 1983
Sandblasted and lampworked
glass, 30 x 14 x 14 in.

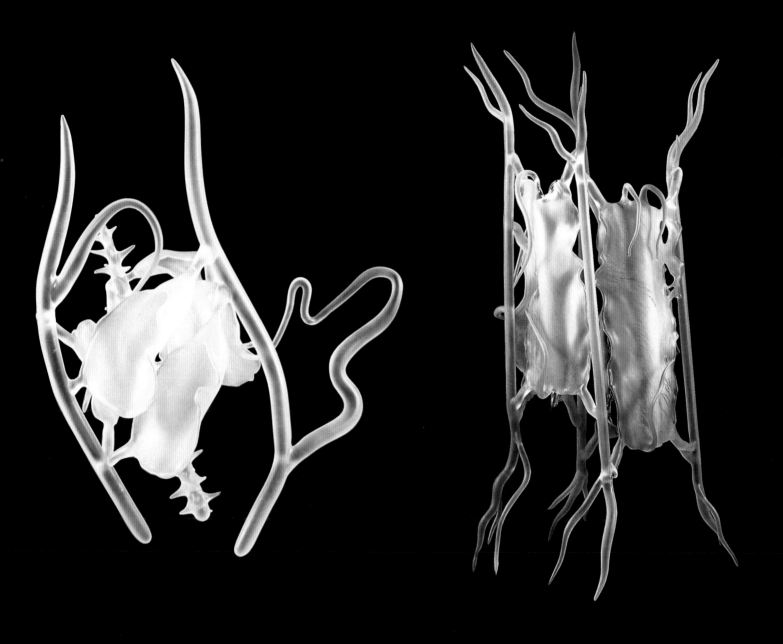

Untitled, 1985
Sandblasted and lampworked
glass, 21 ¾ x 17 x 13 ½ in.
High Museum of Art, Atlanta

Blue Box, 1984
Lampworked glass and
pastel, 25 x 9 x 9 in.

Station 2, 1985
From the installation **Seven Stations
of Intimacy**, Fay Gold Gallery, Atlanta
Neon and fabric, 36 x 96 x 48 in.

$\mathcal{I}n\,\mathcal{D}ecember$ 1984, Ruffner's maternal grandmother died. Ruffner's grief brought about an intense period of self-reflection: "I realized I had this dichotomy in my work. At the time I was making very large, colorful paintings and relatively small, pristine, white glass sculptures. I decided I should synthesize things more and began painting on the glass." One of her first pieces with color, simply called *Ocean Form* (1985), loops out in a low line like a snagged piece of kelp on which wave three small and one large cornucopia-shaped "leaves." This piece and others similar to the Dancing Box Series are shaded in pale pink, blue, and green with pastels and colored pencil. The sandblasted surface holds the applied color, which is blended by rubbing and then sprayed with a fixative.

This transition in the work was followed by a larger one in Ruffner's life: she decided to leave Atlanta to settle in Seattle. During the summer of 1984, she had taught at the Pilchuck Glass School north of Seattle. Despite having to provide all the torches and tools for the students of the fledgling program that first year, she had enjoyed the experience. Seattle offered further summer teaching opportunities at Pilchuck. The area also had a growing, supportive glass community, and its strong public arts program offered an opportunity to try some larger work. So Ruffner loaded up her blue Isuzu pickup truck and headed west.

By July 1986, Seattle's "oyster light" was flooding Ruffner's studio near the Pike Street Market, and all the work took on a new cast—and a new cast of characters. Where abstraction had once been, figures and images began to appear. In a now often quoted statement, she explained:

> That's when I knew my work needed an attitude adjustment. So I walked into the studio and slapped all their faces and began to make user-friendly sculptures that wear too much eye makeup but really know how to have a good time in a bar. They don't stand on pedestals anymore; they dance on tabletops. They keep me up at night carousing. Now that I've dressed them up, they think they can go anywhere, especially if Marcel drives.[4]

She added later, "I think probably there was so much going on in my life at the time that I felt compelled to communicate it, and the only way I felt I could do that was in a method that was more concretely intelligible, open to speculation and interpretation, but with more specific directives for the viewer to know my intention."

Ruffner had chosen glass because its properties and allusional possibilities pleased her. In turn, she chose narrative because imagery offered her a way to be more specific in communicating with her audience. But by choosing glass as a medium and narrative as a mode, Ruffner also became one of the growing group of women artists who were intent on breaking down the barriers between art and craft, rebelling against the notion of art and artist being above any worldly connection:

> I'm not a modernist. I don't believe in the macho concept of the solo genius, alone, making his art. We're human. We exist within a society, and to deny that is absurd. I like absurdity, but that is a bit much for me.

> Artists never work alone. . . . Like it or not, you are influenced by your experience and by your contact with others. If you truly look inside yourself and make your work from that place, you touch on what is human and therefore common. You make the most universal statement by making the most personal ones. It takes a lot of courage to work from that part of you. To make that into art requires more courage than to make art that theoretically exists independent of any human intervention, or art for art's sake.

Ruffner's belief in the universal nature of her own experiences underpins everything that she has created. Her delight in discovery, what she describes as "connecting the dots," is the wellspring for what she has to tell. Her desire to prompt people to see some of what she sees, to get them thinking in a new way, provides the impetus for her work. From these convictions the narrative pieces unfold like stimulating conversation.

Perhaps it was inevitable that her first piece with recognizable imagery contains one of Ruffner's favorite objects—shoes. *The History of Shoes Compared to Postmodern Architecture* (1986, p. 25) related "two things overtrivialized, seemingly decorative, but useful and necessary." Constructed in the outline of a house, the sculpture's centerpieces are a large pink pump and a cloud that offers additional colors and styles of footwear. The glass rod legs of the piece are decorated with what would become perennial Ruffner images—a bow, a building, a chair, fruit, leaves, even a snake. With time, other tripods of glass rods became transformed into blue moons, stars, turnips, and women's legs. The flattened white sides of the boxes evolved into faces or formed canvases for more detailed imagery—pictures of mountains, maps, fish, and dancing chickens.

Imagery became a unique shorthand as Ruffner built her iconography, a veritable alphabet for glassy story lines. Some images were straightforward, some metaphorical, and some were chosen simply because of their shapes or personal connotations for Ruffner. Snakes, for instance, fit all three—as animals, as metaphorical references both in biblical and early goddess mythology, and because "they are such great natural lines." Dice she finds loaded with connotation and graphic appeal; hearts frequently have arrows "because if you have an open heart, you have to realize that it will be vulnerable to all the slings and arrows of outrageous reality." For Ruffner, wings show the transcendent nature of art itself: "All art is inspirational and gives you wings to fly out of your reality into the realm of the imagination; in that realm, everybody can fly."

Throughout the period of 1986 to 1989, Ruffner's lampwork took on its definitive nature. As she added to her imagery, story lines began to fall into themes: answers to unanswerable "what if" questions; romance—or as she put it, "chronicles of Ginny's heart #3012"; what it means to be female; and the what, how, and why of scientific theory. All these inquiries became springboards for pieces whose titles were wildly associative, resonant with allusions and puns: *Ghost Turnips in the Sky, The Tunnel of Love Wears Heartbreak Pajamas, The Birth of Caviar, Beuth & Trudy, How Daylight Savings Time Was Invented, Herman Nootics.* Inspired by Duchamp and her love of words, Ruffner integrated the titles with the pieces, part of the viewer's "take" on the whole:

> **I see the titles as a jumping-off point, a reference for the viewers. If you give them too much, you don't give them an opportunity to participate with the piece and make their own judgments. But if you give a little direction, it is helpful. Susan Sontag had a great line: "Art is seduction, not rape." The idea is that seduction requires complicity. You have to have complicity with the viewers; they have to want to be there. The titles offer them a bottle of wine, good music, and romantic mood setting, an invitation to come on up and see my sculptures.**

As the titles grew more fanciful, Ruffner grew more skillful in sculpting the glass imagery. By 1987 the legs of the lampwork tripod more and more became images instead of being merely decorated with them. For instance, in *The Evolution of the Chicken Tango* (p. 28), Ruffner's first play on the why-did-the-chicken-cross-the-road joke, a dashing yellow and red hen dances daintily, front and center, perched on one ballet-slippered foot. Greek columns flank her left and right, while the third leg of the tripod directly behind the hen is a brilliant orange carrot, its green top flying upward. Arching over the hen are the artist's eye, a hand holding a translucent egg, and a winking blue moon—a punning reference to how often we can expect to find a chicken who tangos while crossing the road.

Throughout the early years in Seattle, there was a growing emphasis on painted imagery and shaping in Ruffner's sculpture. Her early pieces relied on simple tinting. Through experiments with many media, she found she could shade the glass, enhance opacity or translucence, even play with illusional space. *Chicken Tango* illustrates Ruffner's growing skill with color in the tender shading of the hand, which creates a soft roundness while retaining enough transparency that the skin seems luminous.

In another piece from 1987, *The Crabs Herd Pyramids on the Flying M Ranch,* small patterns increase the layers of color and add decorative notes to the linear portions of the sculpture. In time, the concept of pattern itself would lead Ruffner to an entire series, but in the early work, it marked more of a filling-in, an expression of her love of opulence and decoration.

In art circles, "decorative" is often used pejoratively, as if being pleasing to look at makes art less worthy. But Ruffner, who believes that creating beauty is one of the primary reasons for art, also believes that decoration provides one of the languages through which beauty can be conveyed:

> **I wouldn't go so far as to say decoration makes life worth living, but it can transform anything. You can take a plain anything—plain book, cup, building, or vehicle—and the way you decorate it can make it more valuable, and even change its meaning. It is a method of both identification and status. Decoration is a language that tells you things. Decoration is a language I like to be fluent in.**

In addition, the very nature of lampwork is accretive. Unlike stone or wood sculpture, which involves a reductive process, lampwork sculpture is built up. So it was natural for Ruffner, who admits to a ro-coco sensibility, to find her glasswork growing larger and more complex in both form and content. From 1986 to 1988, however, the narrative remained jocular—small dioramas with a quirky playfulness, punch lines to the verbal puns played out in the titles. The fun was seeing if you could get all the double entendres, read the language in the decoration. As a result of this, critics frequently describe Ruffner's work as "whimsical," a term that angers her. It is nomenclature she refuted in the statement she made for her solo show at the Huntington Museum in Huntington, West Virginia, in 1988:

> **Whimsy implies a lack of forethought, a whim. This is serious silly. The roles of the fool and the idiot were sacred roles. Society allowed the fool to point a finger at his nakedness, or to go naked, or any number of usually unacceptable behaviors. The village idiot was the conscience of the town. The artist's holy job is as the conscience of contemporary society. In this fin-de-siècle time, conservative politics demand we lighten up, the disappearing environment demands we pay attention.**

Clearly, though Ruffner was not being satirical, she wanted the viewer to read the underlying ironies. Perhaps it was one reason why by the end of 1989 Ruffner was using shorter, more enigmatic titles, turning increasingly to metaphor and appropriated imagery to carry the connotative layers of her work. Life was getting more complex for her, and though she kept her sense of the absurd, expansion in her work and her growing involvement in the international glass community thrust her into positions of responsibility and serious consideration, which were bound to reverberate in her art.

From the first year Ruffner moved to Seattle, she did not limit herself to lampwork. She began to shape other facets of her career. In 1986 she moved into public art in a collaboration with artist Richard Posner for Bumgardner Architects—a 100-foot underground pedestrian tunnel connecting the Triangle Parking

Garage and the University of Washington Medical Center. They tiled sides of the tunnel with imagery suggesting an arbor. Overhead they placed a wooden trellis. When one walks through the tunnel, song-birds trill and twitter on tape in a continuous morning song. It is easy to identify first-time visitors to the hospital: they are craning their necks, looking for the birds that certainly must be hidden in the trellis.

In 1987 Ruffner completed an outdoor mural 150 feet long by 50 feet high on the remnant of the sup-porting wall of the old post office in downtown Seattle, adjacent to the Harbor Steps that now join First Avenue and Western at University. For this mural Ruffner chose chalk to make the large abstract color fields, a medium that reflected the transitoriness of the remaining bit of structure.

Three shows at the Traver Sutton Gallery in Seattle enlarged upon her painting and installation work: two installations of large sculpture and lampwork, *Dreams That Have Had Me* in 1987, and *Mixo-glossia* in 1988; and another collaboration in 1987, a display of paintings entitled *Shared Secrets*, done with her friend novelist Tom Robbins. These variations on the theme of Ernie Bushmiller's 1930–82 comic strip *Nancy*, played off the "gear-tooth spikes" of Nancy's hair, a form that Robbins described as "simultaneously organic and inorganic, biomorphic and mechanical. . . . It's a primal, mythic shape, rooted in the reptilian reaches of the limbic lobes. And, of course, it has obvious Buddha qualities." [5]

A mugger attacked Ruffner in the alley behind her studio in 1986. The sculptures in *Dreams That Have Had Me* included two pieces that helped Ruffner to exorcise that frightening experience. One was *Dream of the White Horse* (1987), a huge blue boulder of a head over which floats a gold horse with an even smaller green horse balanced between its ears. The other, *Déjà Vu All Over Again* (1986, pp. 26–27), presents two figures locked in a close embrace under an arbor decorated for a party. From the front, the couple is dancing, but from the back, the male figure becomes Death strangling the woman.

The theme of *Mixoglossia* was playful. *The Big Palm Theory* (1988), a hand, nearly 8 feet tall and lit from within, sports Saturn, a large blue eye, and a lemon yellow urn at its fingertips. A fish with glassy scales spouts an orange tornado, and a gold column with wings is *The Landing and the Taking Off* (1988).

When I asked Ruffner why she likes to do larger sculpture, she retorted, "I like to make things that are bigger than me, and I like making things I can kick. You can't kick glass!" Working with others collabo-ratively and on public art projects, however, balances the isolation of her studio work in glass. Painting allows for immediacy. All three offer a chance to play with scale:

> Usually form dictates the size of the sculpture for me. Some forms don't translate well small or, con-versely, large. For example, pencils are great larger. I make them bigger and put them in lampwork pieces, and I make them really huge and put them in public art, but I don't think they work small. I also realized that making things out of glass was only good for part of what I had to say. Public art, especially, allows me to work bigger and encompasses more materials. By altering the size of the things I make, and by juxtaposing them with different objects, I hope to make the viewer pause and think about what he or she is seeing.

In 1989 Ruffner began two of her best-known series in her lampwork sculpture: the still lifes and the adventures of Beauty. Both had deep connections with Ruffner's questioning the male-dominated proscriptions of art history. Both reflected a growing feminism that ironically sprouted from her in-creasing success in the worlds of glass art, sculpture, and public art, all areas where women had not attained prominence.

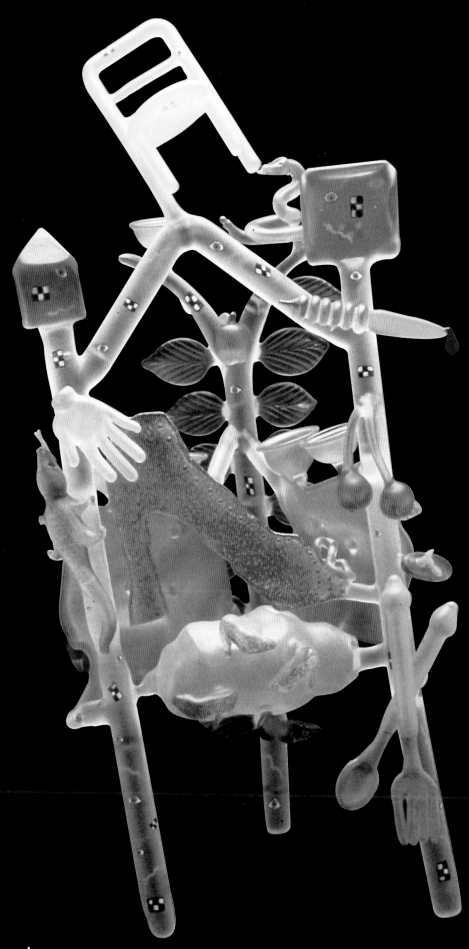

**The History of Shoes Compared
to Postmodern Architecture**, 1986
Lampworked glass and mixed
media, 24 x 12 x 12 in.

(above)
Déjà Vu All Over Again, 1986
(front view) Mixed media
installation at Traver Sutton Gallery,
Seattle, 1987, 12 x 9 x 6 ft.
(right)
Déjà Vu All Over Again, 1986
(back view)

26

**The Evolution of the
Chicken Tango**, 1987
Lampworked glass and mixed
media, 19 x 15 x 12 in.

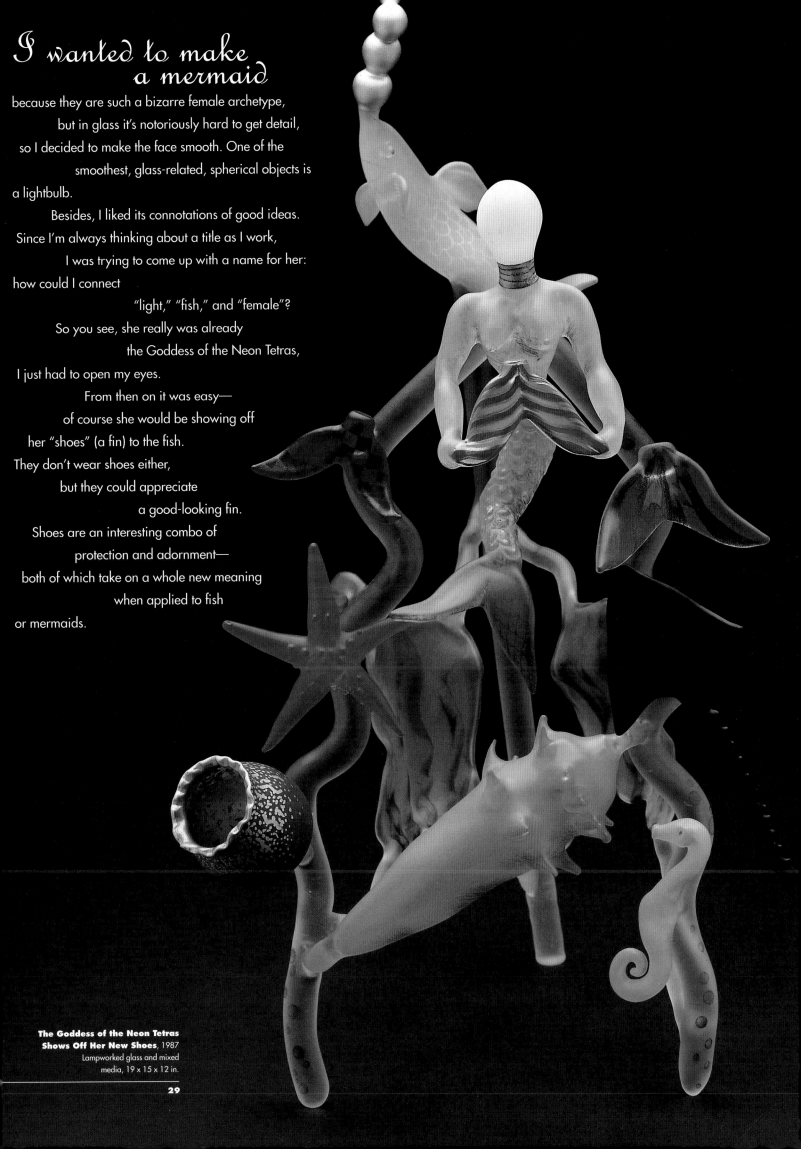

I wanted to make a mermaid

because they are such a bizarre female archetype,
but in glass it's notoriously hard to get detail,
so I decided to make the face smooth. One of the
smoothest, glass-related, spherical objects is
a lightbulb.

Besides, I liked its connotations of good ideas.
Since I'm always thinking about a title as I work,
I was trying to come up with a name for her:
how could I connect
"light," "fish," and "female"?
So you see, she really was already
the Goddess of the Neon Tetras,
I just had to open my eyes.
From then on it was easy—
of course she would be showing off
her "shoes" (a fin) to the fish.
They don't wear shoes either,
but they could appreciate
a good-looking fin.
Shoes are an interesting combo of
protection and adornment—
both of which take on a whole new meaning
when applied to fish
or mermaids.

**The Goddess of the Neon Tetras
Shows Off Her New Shoes**, 1987
Lampworked glass and mixed
media, 19 x 15 x 12 in.

Architecture Frying in Succotash Hell, 1988
Lampworked glass and mixed media, 21 x 17 x 15 in. Collection of Mr. and Mrs. David Wolf

My Pickup Truck in the Garden of Eden, 1988
Lampworked glass and
mixed media, 21 x 22 x 17 in.
Collection of Gary MacPherson

Underwater Florist, 1988
Lampworked glass and mixed
media, 24 x 13 x 13 in. Collection
of Samuel and Althea Stroum

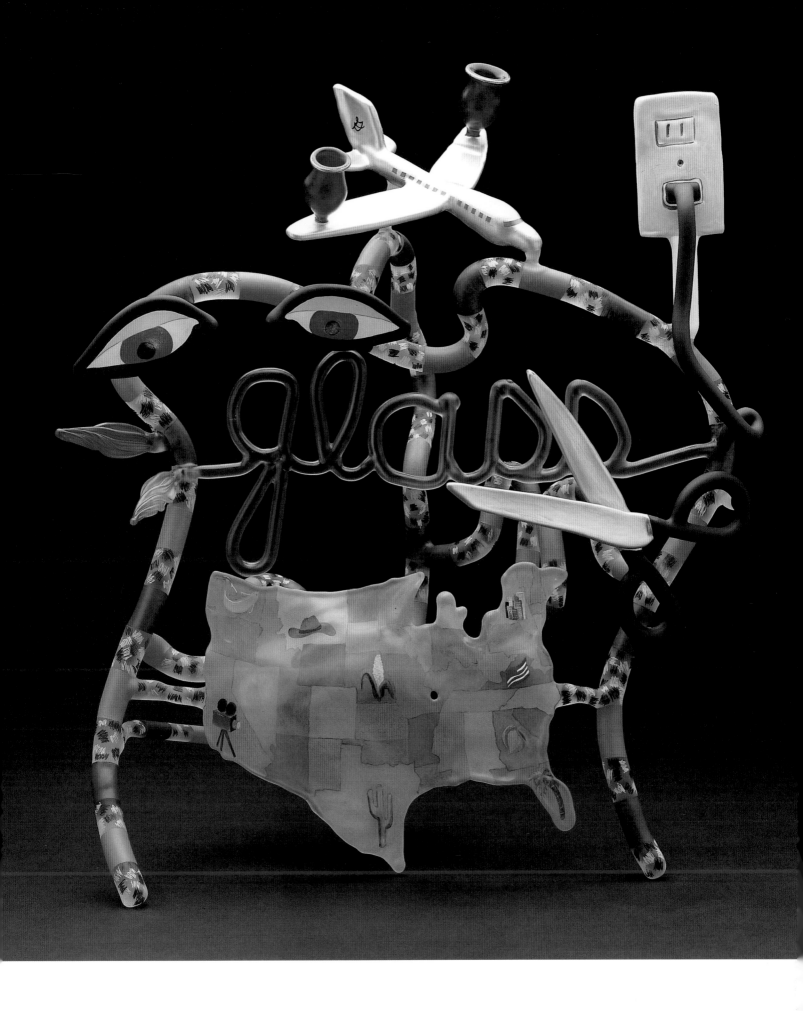

Glass America Coupon, 1988
Lampworked glass and mixed
media, 24 x 33 x 11 in.

In 1988 Ruffner made a lampwork piece, entitled *Arguing with Men over the State of My Soul,* with the figure of a dove carrying pearls and the head of a man with golden bows streaming in symbolic condescension from his mouth. It was the outcome of an article she had written earlier that year for *American Craft* in which she asked sculptors, educators, critics, and others within and outside glass art why they thought there were so few women making sculpture in glass and in general.[6] Ruffner later amplified her ideas:

> One of the issues that I didn't get to address [in the article] was that there aren't many good role models for women artists. The artist's sense of connection with the artistic mythos by its very essence comes from the subconscious. You may say, "Well, I don't need it anyway," but you do. You need that canon whether good or bad, to have a point of departure.

> When I talk or write about the difficulty women artists have, I hear, "What are you complaining about? You're in every show; you get commissions." That I'm doing all right doesn't mean that problems for women artists don't exist. It means that it's my responsibility, since I have a little more visibility, to point that out.

Simply by her use of narrative, autobiography, decoration, and craft, Ruffner sides artistically with much thinking that the more radical feminism in the art of the 1970s and 1980s emphasized.[7] Unlike many feminists, however, Ruffner dislikes dictating conclusions to her audience, which stops her from making didactic art. She does not claim to promote a feminist agenda in her work but, rather, in the way she conducts herself as an artist. Her inquiry into that role, however, is at times subversively feminist as she revises and comments upon the historic role of women in art.

An ongoing form of that inquiry emerges in Ruffner's still lifes. In their presentation, they are as formalized and prosaic as their counterparts in paintings—an intimate scene developed around a bottle of wine, luscious-looking fruit, flowers, and the suggestion of a tabletop, all with limited depth of field. Though her still lifes are three dimensional, Ruffner keeps them purposely flat and frontal to echo the familiar format in drawing and painting. Bottles and wine glasses aren't blown forms but outlines or painted flat surfaces. Rarely straightforward, the still lifes frequently contain visual jokes or puns in their titles to push us into new considerations. In one of the earliest pieces of this series, a bottle of wine, with a banana, apple, and pear on an illusionally off-balance stemmed server, sits on a table swimming with grinning rainbow trout. Frozen in its glassy moment, the piece is appropriately entitled *Stilled Life* (1989, p. 48). Another, with similar components but with less jocular Piscean forms, became *Still Glass* (1989, p. 39). The still life joined another favorite image of Ruffner's, the skyscraper, in *Still Life with Architecture* (1989, p. 44), and violated decorum with an insolent flower, leaves brashly on hips, in *Not So Still Life* (1990).

Ruffner revises the still life to exploit its instant allusion to art history and to open discussion of the limitations women artists faced in the past:

> Still lifes were traditionally an acceptable subject for women to paint. They were supposedly safer than the alternative—painting nudes. But still lifes are sexy, too, because fecundity is always implied. In addition, I think that the fruit is female, growing and changing, beautiful and nutritious, functional. So I paint them to provoke conversation about all that.

Whereas still lifes continue to arise periodically in Ruffner's art, her Beauty Series, begun in late 1989, ran an intense course for one year and then was finished. But it spurred Ruffner to reflect on the multiple aspects of the question of beauty and to use it as an ongoing theme.

The figure of Beauty was a sassy descendant of her own sublime great-grandmother, the Greek statue *Nike of Samothrace*. Ruffner's Beauty also has wings but no head or arms, and sports an updated tunic with a short skirt. A Ruffner alter ego, she first appeared balanced gracefully on a dinosaur skeleton for a steed in *Beauty Learning from the Past* (1989), took a quick slide through the still life series in *Beauty Surfing through a Still Life* (1989, p. 42), and immediately began to have adventures with mythological and real beauties frequently depicted in art. *Beauty as Salome* (1990) danced with John the Baptist's head on a platter; *Beauty as Athena, Eve, and Pandora* (1990, p. 49) posed on a skeleton, toes touching the part of man from which they had emerged in their origin myths. Beauty also adventured with art concepts—being created by art, acting with drama, costuming herself as the Muses. Sometimes she took control, moving into art's neighborhood, lassoing the tornado of the heart, deconstructing portraiture. Her presence, for Ruffner, provided a point of continuity in the narrative questioning, which had become more succinct and thus needed a quicker visual metaphor. "I realized if I had a thread, a recurring element or figure, the viewer would recognize it and ask 'What is she doing this time?' I could put her in different situations and she could take on different personas." The narrative began to run among individual pieces like a dialogue.

Beauty appeared in changing form and was disassembled as wall sculpture in Ruffner's 1990 installation at William Traver Gallery in Seattle. In *The Pursuit of Beauty: Thesis*, her torso, an armature covered in glass, hung below a single white wing. In 1991 she disappeared with *The Last of the Beauties* (p. 73), a circle of Beauty figures with scenes through windows for faces, an artistic relative of the poetic metaphor of the eye being the window of the soul.

Wherever Beauty went, she explored the female perspective on art. And as with the still lifes, she insisted that though men and the art world of the twentieth century might not understand her approach to the world—her love of opulence and decoration, her penchant for seeking connections rather than separations—such a world view just might be viable. Ruffner's work on this series, however, took her beyond championing feminism. She continues to be curious about the concept of beauty, its role in art, and its influence on the artist as well as the viewer, and much of her work from 1990 through the present explores this topic.

"I have had an ongoing fascination with the concept of beauty," explains Ruffner, "both as an artist and as a female. What is beauty? What makes something beautiful? It is culturally and temporally defined, yet how is that conveyed? How do we teach this to our youth, educate people as to what is beautiful, and how do we determine it in the first place?" Ruffner's search for answers mines the field she knows best, the history of art. In the past, beauty has often been art's raison d'être, but in the twentieth century, beauty's virtue has been questioned. Scorned by modernists who associated beauty with representation or decoration, and targeted by politically correct postmodernists, beauty in contemporary art has fallen into disrepute, reduced to "mereness"—merely pretty, merely decorative.

For Ruffner, the role of beauty in art is an issue worthy of discourse. She explores it with humor, imagery, and a discreet disregard for general opinion. For instance, nearly a third of her sculptures from 1989 through 1993 carry an appropriated image of a famous beauty figure. *La Donna Mobile*

(1990, back cover) frames a close-up of Botticelli's famed blonde from *Birth of Venus* (ca. 1480); in *The Sources of Creativity* (1991, p. 60) five hands hold symbols of art history—a landscape, fruit, flowers, architecture, and portraiture (the *Mona Lisa*). These references achieve layers of association. They are instantly recognizable as symbols of female beauty and fine art. Juxtaposed with pattern or domestic references such as fruit and flowers, they can connote feminine enterprise, postmodern rebellion against modernist progressive principles, or celebration of fecundity and sexuality with an ironic allusion to men's assigning women artists to execute "safe" subjects. All this is incorporated in sculptures that are themselves beautiful objects, rich in the play of paint on glass, light, transparency, and space.

Even when a Ruffner piece is difficult to decipher, it is arresting, tugging us from title to sculpture and back again, suggesting ways of entering into the conversation. In his popular book *Care of the Soul*, Thomas Moore asserts that we often assume beauty is only an accessory to life, dispensable. We don't understand the many ways it feeds the soul:

> The soul is nurtured by beauty. What food is to the body, arresting, complex, and pleasing images are to the soul. If we have a psychology rooted in a medical view of human behavior and emotional life, then the primary value will be health. But if our idea of psychology is based on the soul, then the goal of our therapeutic efforts will be beauty. I will go so far as to say that if we lack beauty in our lives, we will probably suffer familiar disturbances in the soul—depression, paranoia, meaninglessness, and addiction. . . .

> If we are going to care for the soul, and if we know that the soul is nurtured by beauty, then we will have to understand beauty more deeply and give it a more prominent place in life.[8]

Ruffner's work addresses this understanding of beauty, and in pursuing this theme, she achieves it.

Two other qualities developed in Ruffner's work in the early 1990s. One was a growing complexity of form, and the other was an intensification of painted pattern. Pattern runs riot in *Wild Indian* (1991, p. 61). A maze of decorated glass rods, with feather-shaped ends arching across the top, it hits the eye with a war whoop of yellow, orange, blue, green, and red. Pattern is everywhere—suggestions of Miró, Kandinsky, Picasso, painted on the feathers—but it exists within the lines of the lampwork as well, the bends and elbows repeating shape and line.

"I like Klee and Kandinsky," states Ruffner. "I like their use of color, their use of line, their repetition, their rhythm, their syncopation. I think they know a lot about pictorial space and walking the line between representation and abstraction."

During this period Ruffner achieved another type of complexity through recontextualization, with references to classical portraiture—Manet, Vermeer, David—interposed among fruit and flowers and pieces of pattern from Picasso or Miró, as in *When a Still Life Dreams* (p. 62) and *Flower/Finger* (p. 64), or mixed with Ruffner's own iconography, as in *Serpent Harp* (p. 65), all of 1991. As pattern and appropriation became predominant in the work, biographical references grew more oblique, mirroring a greater need for inner privacy as Ruffner, her life becoming increasingly public, moved out into the world on all fronts.

Ruffner reached an apex of productivity between 1989 and 1991. She created nearly 100 lampwork sculptures, which found homes in such far-flung places as the Hokkaido Museum of Modern

Art, Sapporo, Japan, the Queensland Art Gallery, Queensland, Australia, and the Cathedral of St. Denis at Tourtour, France. She had two solo installations—*The Pursuit of Beauty* (p. 46) at William Traver Gallery in Seattle in 1989, and *The Possession of Creativity* (p. 52) at the Renwick Gallery in Washington, D.C., in 1990. Ruffner also went to Italy to design and supervise the off-hand sculpture (work formed on a blowpipe or punty rod by bringing bits of hot glass from the furnace) and blowing of eleven large glass designs for the Vistosi factory of Murano (p. 45). In addition, she was commissioned to do a piece for an advertisement in the artists' series of Absolut Vodka (it was photographed as a hologram), produced a solo show of her paintings for Linda Farris Gallery in Seattle, and completed commissioned designs for five public art projects.

The paintings are rich depictions of various kinds of fruit with lush-sounding names—"chaumontel pear," "pitmaston orange nectarine," "black tartarian cherry." Carefully placed on oversized backdrops of aluminum, mahogany, or gold-painted canvas, they speak of opulence and fecundity, overlapping metaphors from the lampwork. Those painted on aluminum in particular play with light and the yin/yang of hard and soft, nature and technology. In a 1990 interview, Ruffner said of her painting, "It gives me a lot of joy, and there is no purpose to it at all." But clearly it has been incorporated as a continuing facet of her oeuvre. Says Ruffner now, "I like paint: the smell, feel, look—the total experience of painting—as well as the result. But being a painter is an indefensible job. It's hard to convince anybody of your value to society. I know it is absolutely integral and necessary, but it is very difficult to convince the general masses why society needs painters."

Of the public art designs, three were realized and carried to completion. The first, in 1988, part of the redesign of South Park Community Center, a park and multiuse building in one of Seattle's neighborhoods near Boeing Field, was the most elaborate (pp. 40–41). Here the goal was to keep the feel of the old center and to tie into the makeup of the community, an ethnic mix of Hispanic, African American, Asian, and Caucasian. Ruffner focused on the children, creating a fanciful arching gate of cut metal with oversized images connected to the park and neighborhood: a baseball bat, a grinning sun, a window with an urn pouring out a fish (a reference to the nearby Duwamish waterway), and the name of the park done in a style reminiscent of lacy Mexican cut paperwork. A game-board walkway stretches under the gate and into the lobby of the building, its squares containing 1,000 bronze inserts of planets, local landmarks, animals, numbers, and the alphabet, rendered in letters, braille, and sign language. Ruffner also had to consider the problem of durability in the decoration of two locker rooms. She resolved the twin dilemma of possible breakage and defacement by making tiles with the handprints of famous local athletes side-by-side with those of the children from the neighborhood.

The second commission, in 1990, offered a more sublime site, the exterior of the Security Pacific Gallery in downtown Seattle (pp. 56–57). For this Ruffner created huge bronze wings that flew upward along the facade above the door to the gallery, then around the side of the structure as though the building itself might transcend its worldly orientation and fly away.

The third, not completed until 1993, was a playground "oasis" for the Machan Primary School in Phoenix, Arizona, and included a shaded seating area, water fountain, and game-board play areas beneath a steel mesh canopy topped with colorful cutouts including a red question mark, a spider's web, a yellow sunflower, and a giant magnifying glass (pp. 86–87).

Of the public art Ruffner says, "I wanted to make something that was permanent and could be enjoyed by more than a few. Being a responsible part of the community, it's hard for me to justify to myself making only art which gets bought by a select few and sequestered."

Ruffner's need to contribute in more public arenas also led her to serve on a variety of art boards, commissions, and societies. She served on the Seattle Art Commission and the Pilchuck Glass School board of trustees, was on the board of directors and eventually president of the Glass Art Society, and also served as their annual conference coordinator when they met in Seattle in 1990. That same year she was a juror for *New Glass Review 11,* sponsored by the Corning Museum of Glass, served on the editorial advisory board for *Glass* magazine, and in 1991 curated *Glass: Material in the Service of Meaning,* a conceptually based exhibition, for the Tacoma Art Museum. When I asked her how she was able to do so much, she said: "I worked ten hours a day, seven days a week."

That was until Sunday, December 22, 1991.

Still Glass, 1989
Lampworked glass and mixed
media, 17 x 14 x 8 in.

Entry Portal, 1989
South Park Community Center, Seattle
Painted steel, 26 x 21 x 3 ft.

**Beauty Surfing
through a Still Life**, 1989
Lampworked glass and mixed
media, 9 x 14 x 9 in.

42

Beauty Fleeing the Raft of the Medusa, 1989
Lampworked glass and mixed media, 14 x 14 x 11 in.

43

Still Life with Architecture, 1989
Lampworked glass and mixed
media, 12 x 13 x 6 in.

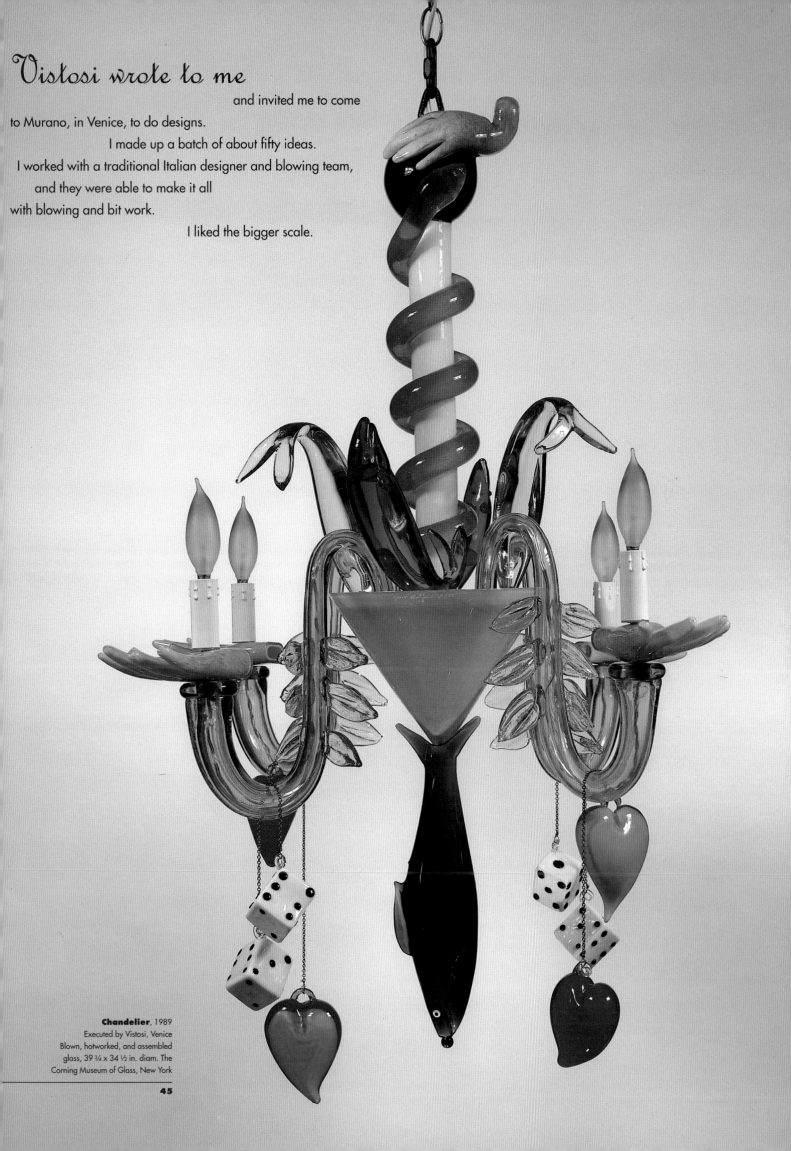

Vistosi wrote to me and invited me to come to Murano, in Venice, to do designs. I made up a batch of about fifty ideas. I worked with a traditional Italian designer and blowing team, and they were able to make it all with blowing and bit work. I liked the bigger scale.

Chandelier, 1989
Executed by Vistosi, Venice
Blown, hotworked, and assembled
glass, 39 ¾ x 34 ½ in. diam. The
Corning Museum of Glass, New York

45

The Pursuit of Beauty, 1989
Installation at William Traver Gallery, Seattle
Glass and mixed media, dimensions
variable. Collection of the artist

Stilled Life, 1989
Lampworked glass and mixed
media, 13 x 14 x 8 in.

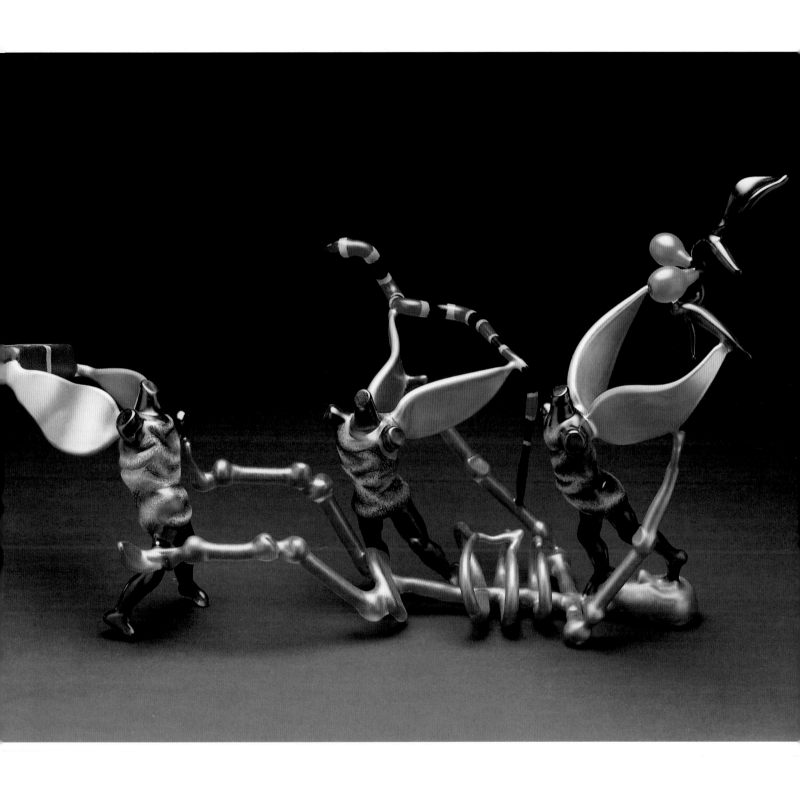

**Beauty as Athena,
Eve, and Pandora**, 1990
Lampworked glass and mixed
media, 14 x 25 x 20 in.

Beauty, Caravaggio's Medusa, is regarding

herself in the mirror. What she sees is Botticelli's Venus.

The mirror she's holding is framed with snakes.

This piece is about the value and power of self-love

as well as about the power of the mind to control perception.

Beauty as Medusa, 1990
Lampworked glass and mixed media,
22 x 25 x 19 in. (variable)

**Beauty Being
Created by Art**, 1990
Lampworked glass and mixed
media, 11 x 20 x 15 in.

Can creativity be possessed?

Doesn't it possess you?

As an artist, if you give yourself over to creativity

—don't resist it—

it gains strength within you, becoming an irresistible force,

like a tornado.

That is why I chose to put a tornado as

the central image.

It's a scary force, but very beautiful,

which is why it is covered with glass drops.

In the installation there is also

a sequence of three paintings in which

a very beautiful female angel materializes

out of a tornado

and then returns.

This installation was also about beauty.

The Possession of Creativity, 1990
Installation at Renwick Gallery,
Smithsonian Institution, Washington, D.C.
Steel, glass, and oil on canvas,
20 x 50 x 30 ft.

**Beauty Develops the
Picture Plane: A**, 1990
From the installation **The Possession
of Creativity**, Renwick Gallery,
Smithsonian Institution, Washington, D.C.
Oil on canvas, 8 x 10 ft.

54

**Beauty Develops the
Picture Plane: B**, 1990
From the installation **The Possession
of Creativity**, Renwick Gallery,
Smithsonian Institution, Washington, D.C.
Oil on canvas, 10 x 13 ft.
Collection of the artist

At the time this was commissioned and installed,
the space was the corporate gallery.

I wanted to make something that would not only celebrate this noble endeavor
of a corporation but would also somehow
signal the unusual use of this normal-looking building.

I decided that wings
would be appropriate because I feel that art lifts you and lets you transcend the everyday.
So if I could suggest either that the building may take

flight

or that there was
some large winged thing inside the building,
it would be a fitting metaphor.

Bronze Wings, 1990
Installation at Security
Pacific Gallery, Seattle
Bronze and aluminum panels
Wings: 18 x 8 ft. ea.
Panels: 2 ½ x 12 ft. ea.

**Beauty as the
Vices and Virtues**, 1990
Lampworked glass and mixed
media, 12 x 10 x 10 in. ea.

Stella at the Louvre, 1990
Lampworked glass and mixed
media, 17 x 16 x 9 in.

Creativity is often manifested through the hands, so this is five hands

holding five different manifestations of creativity—

painting (the *Mona Lisa*),

Nature's beauty (a flower),

architecture (a building),

Nature's productivity (a peach),

and the landscape (a window).

All the hands are offering their gifts rather than grasping them.

The Sources of Creativity, 1991
Lampworked glass and mixed
media, 10 x 8 x 6 in. ea.

Wild Indian, 1991
Lampworked glass and mixed
media, 22 x 27 x 22 in.

We assume that only humans

or only animate beings dream.

I think that's awfully presumptive.

Who's to say

that rocks don't have extended philosophical discussions

or that planets don't flirt?

When a Still Life Dreams, 1991
Lampworked glass and mixed
media, 15 x 28 x 16 in.

This one is a crossover title in that
the first part comes from a literal, visual description,
and the second part is more what I feel when I look at it.
In other words, I feel that the floating figure who is looking back at the viewer seems,
by that look,
to be proposing that the viewer truly interact by entering the pictorial space,
and that there be a reversal of roles—
that the figure in the piece
could become the viewer.

This one is a crossover title in that

Red Flower Falling Back (Come in I Want to Watch You), 1991
Lampworked glass and mixed media,
18 x 32 x 14 in. Collection of the artist

Flower/Finger, 1991
Lampworked glass and mixed media,
25 x 21 x 16 in. Collection of
Mr. and Mrs. Jack Minner

Serpent Harp, 1991
Lampworked glass and mixed media,
19 x 20 x 10 in. Collection of
Anna and Joe Mendel

**The Invention of Games (You
Shouldn't Bet on Reclining)**, 1991
Lampworked glass and mixed
media, 25 x 37 x 20 in. Collection
of Jon and Mary Shirley

66

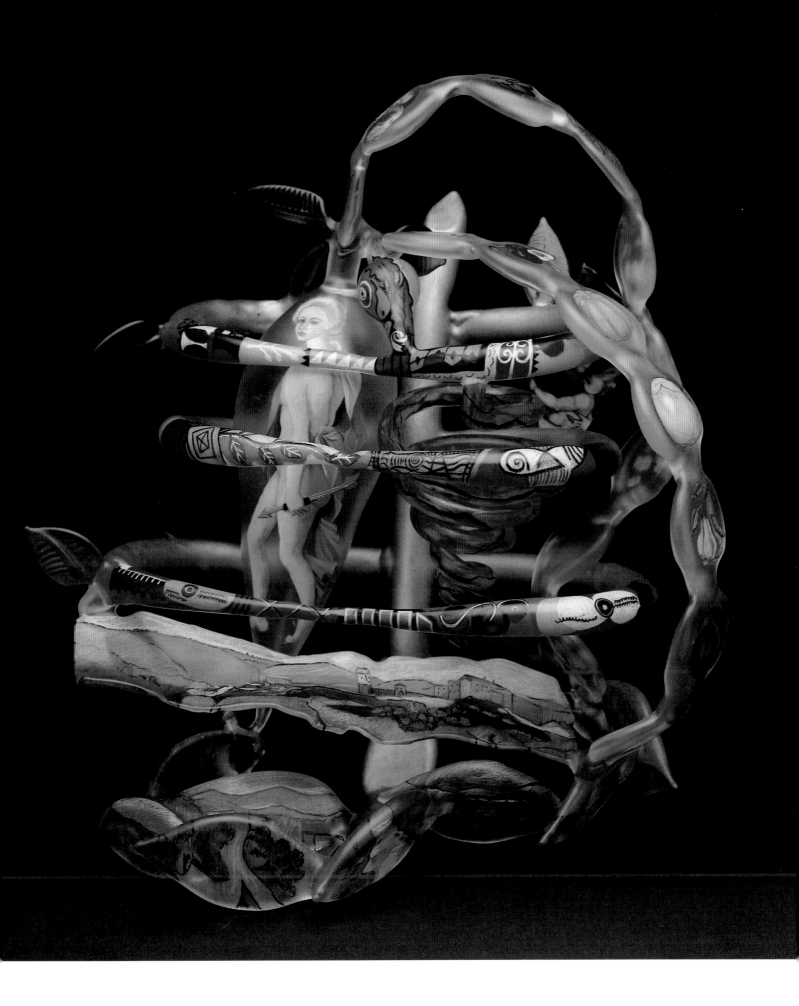

**Protect Your Inner
Landscape**, 1991
Lampworked glass and mixed
media, 16 x 16 x 16 in.

Wilmot's Early Red
Gooseberry, Bright Gold, 1991
Oil on mahogany, 84 x 48 in.

**Red Roman Nectarine,
Pale Gold**, 1991
Oil on canvas, 96 x 72 in.

May Duke Cherry,
Bright Gold, 1991
Oil on canvas, 96 x 72 in.

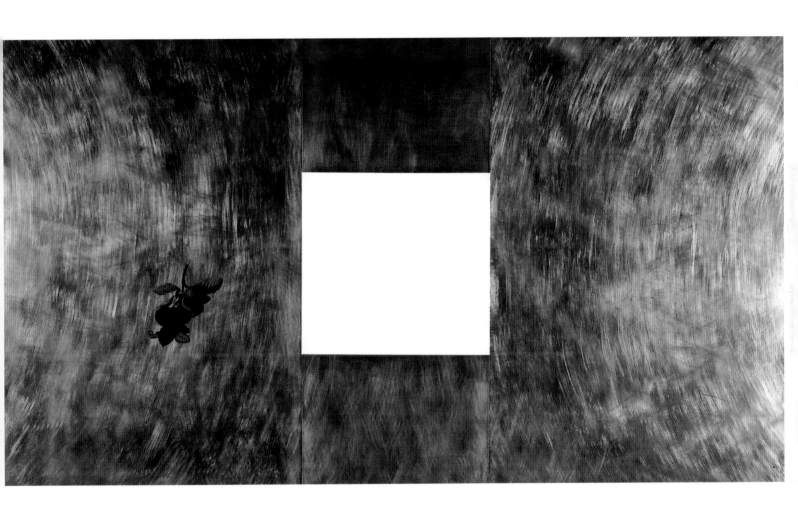

Nectarine, Plum, Aluminum, 1991
Oil on aluminum, 72 x 126 in.

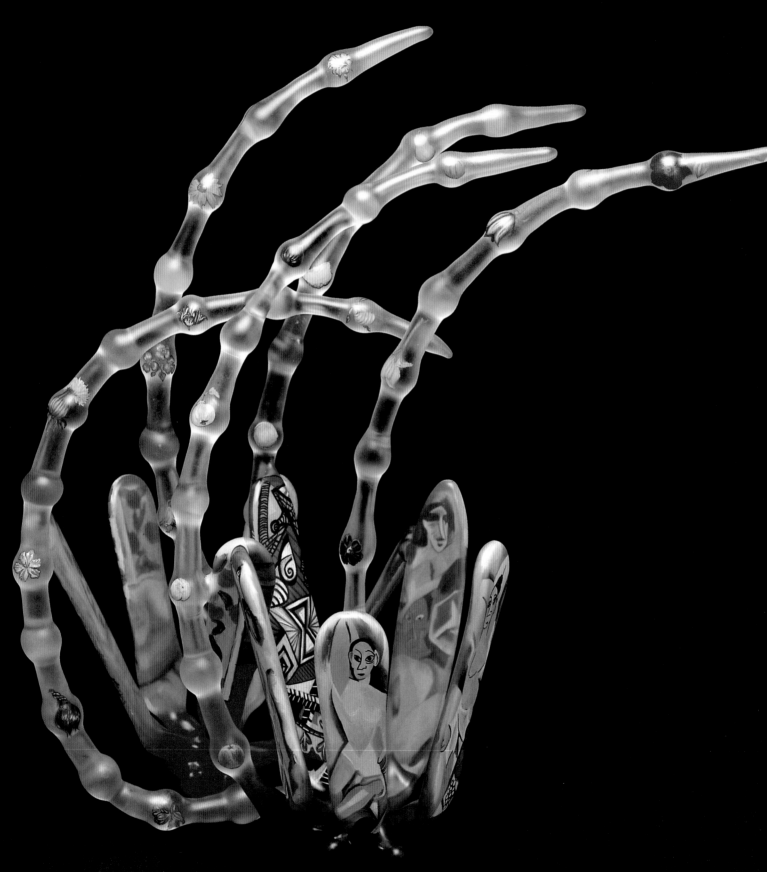

Art Reigns, 1991
Lampworked glass and mixed media,
26 x 24 x 20 in. Collection of the artist

The Last of the Beauties, 1991
Lampworked glass and mixed
media, 13 x 24 x 24 in.

${\cal W}hen\ you\ talk$ to Ruffner, she simply refers to what happened that day in North Carolina as "the wreck." She had gone home for the holiday season and her brother's wedding. Ruffner, with her usual habit of taking care of more than one thing at a time, had gone up to Charlotte for an interview and to prepare for a museum show. When she was late returning, the family went without her to the party to which they had all been invited. But her sister Kay began to worry as time went on and Ruffner didn't come. With no other options, she finally called the hospital. There had been an accident. A car had come onto the freeway at high speed, cutting straight across both lanes of traffic and in front of Ruffner's car. Ruffner had been forced across the deep ditch of the median and into oncoming traffic. Two cars hit her. The impact—despite her wearing a seat belt—threw her to the floor.

People stopped. Firefighters returning from another emergency were flagged down. She was unconscious and not breathing. The firefighters performed an emergency procedure to get air to her lungs and rushed her to the hospital.

Ruffner had no visible broken bones or lacerations except for a small, deep cut on her forehead. But behind the cut, within her skull, the left and right lobes of her brain had sheared, disrupting brain function, shutting down consciousness.

When the family arrived at the hospital, the doctors were not encouraging. They didn't think Ruffner would make it. They asked if she had a living will. The family didn't know of one, so Ruffner, now in a coma, was put on life support. As Mrs. Martin, Ruffner's mother said, "She looked so perfect and whole, as though she were just asleep. We couldn't have done anything differently. It was the start of a long vigil."

Ruffner was stabilized but showed no signs of coming out of the coma. Mrs. Martin credits one of the nurses caring for her daughter with getting Ruffner sent to a rehabilitation hospital: "One nurse kept saying, 'I know someone is in there.' She would pound on Ginny's sternum and felt she saw a flicker. She kept after the doctors until finally they sent Ginny over to rehabilitation." There, after five long weeks, Ruffner began slowly to wake up.

"People think you just wake up, but it is like swimming back into consciousness," explains Ruffner. "It takes several weeks. I have some early memories of opening my eyes and seeing people, but I really don't remember much before about May. I was in and out." One of her first memories of consciousness is of opening her eyes and seeing her partner, Steve Kursh, and her ex-husband standing together at the end of her bed. "I thought, 'They're right; there is a hell,' and did what anyone would do: I closed my eyes and pretended to be asleep!"

No one knew for sure how much damage had been done to her brain. "When I woke up, I couldn't talk or even make a sound. That was hard because neither one of my hands worked well, so I couldn't click my fingers or clap my hands. All I could do was stamp my foot." Kursh recalls that once she regained more arm movement, they gave her a spelling board to answer their questions. But she pointed to strange combinations of words and letters. Ruffner remembers, too, how she finally broke through the miscommunication: "I had really bad double vision, so I would point to letters, but it wouldn't make any sense. Then one day Steve asked me to spell something, and I kept pointing to the wrong letter. He said, 'Are you nuts?' I put two fingers up by my eyes. He said, 'Can't you see?' He figured it out." Once the care team knew it was a matter of sight and not loss of reasoning ability, they approached her problems differently, and Ruffner began to recover more rapidly.

Every day there was work on physical recovery: moving limbs, turning over, getting muscles weak with disuse to function again. Ruffner remembers the first time they gave her physical therapy on her stomach and tried to get her to roll over. "I had been on my back for months. It took four of them. It was awful. I cried, not because it hurt but with the frustration of it all."

Speech was doubly difficult because of the brain injury and a tracheotomy that had injured her larynx. The first made it mentally difficult to retrieve words as well as physically difficult to control the muscles of her throat and tongue; the second affected volume. In time speech returned, but it was slow, slurred, and whispered—hard for listeners to hear and follow, harder yet for Ruffner, who loves to talk and make jokes. For a long time, she couldn't even make the sound of laughter. "I no longer can talk as much as I like, and I can't usually talk about complicated concepts because people can't understand what I say, so I have to keep it simple. Very, very frustrating."

The struggle to relearn to move and talk was uppermost for Ruffner during her time in the hospital. She had no idea what the future held. There was so much to recover. Her parents came to visit her every day to encourage her. They would help her walk up and down the hall, take her out to eat, answer the phone, and translate for her when necessary. When she was eventually able to receive therapy as an outpatient, they took her home with them and drove the fifty-mile round trip to Charlotte each day to take her to therapy.

Seeing her daily improvement was heartening, but they were concerned about what level of recovery could actually be achieved with such a severe injury, or how long it might take. They decided it would be best to send Ruffner's brother out to Seattle to close her studio and move everything into her apartment there for the time being. When they told Ruffner, however, she was furious. "I said, 'Forget the apartment, I want the studio.'" Kursh understood how deeply Ruffner felt about being an artist and knew hope of working again would aid her recovery. He brought her a book of botanical illustrations so she could practice copying them.

When she finally was released from the hospital in late May, she was able to take care of personal needs, to dress herself, and to speak well enough to communicate with those close to her. She had learned to navigate in her wheelchair, but she could not use her left arm or walk, and chewing and swallowing were difficult. Kursh brought her out to Seattle to see the studio, "to let her know who she was," because in many ways, she had forgotten. The way Ruffner describes it, it was like having selective amnesia:

> When I "woke up," I was like a tabula rasa, or like a computer that got shut off before some files were saved. The hard drive was there, although hard to access, but the stuff on the screen was all erased. I still have no recollection of several weeks around the accident. In retrospect, I knew who I was, but I didn't know much about me.
>
> I knew I was an artist. The visual, though difficult—I still have double vision—continued to be my main way of gaining information even about myself. I had no idea what I liked: I could look at my clothes and tell what my taste was, but food? I had no idea. I do remember wanting a burger—and I had been a vegetarian for five years! I was surprised at certain things—movies, movie stars, fashions, events, and places that were at the fore of popular culture. I didn't understand the appeal. There was a period of time when I couldn't bear to watch TV: they could all walk. But the not knowing what I liked was the strangest. In the middle of all this I turned forty. I was just out of the hospital three

weeks. I had always heard that life begins at forty. I took them a little too seriously. I think of myself as someone who has a good imagination, yet I could never have imagined this situation, even in a million years.

In June 1991, Ruffner and Kursh moved back to New York. They would get up, do the *New York Times* crossword puzzle together over breakfast, Kursh asking for words, Ruffner responding, then begin the work day. This meant two hours of therapy sessions for Ruffner, but she also spent time figuring out ways to continue her art work. Kursh bought a computer, and the two of them explored how to use it for designing work. Ruffner also convinced him to stretch a large canvas so she could paint. Now she had to learn to work with her right hand alone because the left was so compromised by the accident. Even then, lack of muscle tone caused her right hand to waver so they attached two-pound ankle weights to her wrist to steady it. When the painting was completed in February 1993, Ruffner wrote in a letter: "I recently completed a 4 by 9 foot pear painting (old style—very realistic—on a gold background). I painted it with my right hand mostly just to prove to myself I could do it, and to remind myself that neither creativity nor skill are located in an appendage."

In the same letter she spoke of completing the Machan School commission in Phoenix, where she had gone in person to oversee the installation. "I wanted to send you a photo of me," she commented, "telling the boys what to do during the installation, but I can't find one. I figure as long as I can talk on the phone and boss boys around, I can get anything done."

Ruffner has used assistants in her studio to help paint the lampwork since 1985. She frequently has to explain that this is not a new tradition in art, citing Michelangelo and Raphael as just two of many artists who hired others to help them realize their creations. She has no patience with those who impute that such an arrangement lessens the value of the work:

> I use my assistants as tools: very talented, smart tools. I only hire artists, and I look at it as a two-way street. I try to help them in their careers any way I can. I have no patience for those who insinuate that using assistants is somehow cheating. Often it is a physical necessity. Obviously, in my case I must have help, but often, when an artist is successful, the demands become just too much. Most importantly, there is, in art as in any other occupation, an awful lot of sheer "busy work."

One of Ruffner's key assistants, Australian lampworker James Minson, fell into the job literally by accident in 1989. He had met Ruffner at Pilchuck and was staying at her studio for a few days while she was out of town. He recalls:

> I kicked a piece that was on the floor and broke it. I attempted to repair it, and it just got worse and worse. I was stubborn because I had broken this piece and I knew Ginny was going to be pissed off, so I kept working at repairing it. Eventually I reconstructed it, made a whole new one. Ginny came back, saw the piece, and thought it was wonderful. So I started making some parts and she'd pay me. It was like a part-time thing. Within a few months, I started putting together whole pieces, still with Ginny [doing the design] but without her having to do any of the physical work. And then she had that car accident. Even so, I guess we were both lucky. Working for Ginny enabled me to get a green card and to stay in the States to do my own work; and now she has someone to make the sculptures for her who knows what she wants and how to do them.

Painter and sculptor Deborah Dohne, who worked for Ruffner before as well as after her accident, says their relationship has been symbiotic:

> I give things out of my work to hers and I get energy back for my own. We've worked together long enough that she trusts me and lets me make technical choices in the give-and-take of the execution. People ask me, don't I want credit for what I do here, but it doesn't feel like my work. The only one I want credit from is Ginny herself. She's very supportive and encourages her assistants in their own work. She's clearly interested; it's not just for show.

Without using assistants, Ruffner could not be nearly as prolific as she is. The loyalty and flexibility of her team enabled her to again create her lampwork sculpture, seven months after the accident.

Ruffner had a show scheduled at Heller Gallery in New York for the fall of 1993, and so had a goal to work toward. At first it was primarily to finish pieces she had already begun. She would design on the computer or simply write descriptions to Dohne and Minson, faxing instructions back and forth. Once new pieces got underway, they shipped the unfinished work to New York, where Ruffner and her assistants there finished it.

The show at Heller Gallery was aptly titled *When Consciousness Sleeps (Where Does It Go?)*. The work was vintage Ruffner, but the cover piece for the catalogue showed the first tentative probing of current concerns. *The Secrets of Eye Hand Coordination* (1993, p. 82) is a pyramid of hands with eyes painted on the palms. At the top is a vulnerable heart pierced with arrows; descending one side are two pudgy angels holding hearts, arrows, and purses. Below, a round of high cards—a lucky draw—offers a circle of support.

As 1993 progressed, more and more of the work came to reflect a new perspective on old themes. Ruffner's interest in science became focused on the origins of thought patterns and how the brain works. Questions regarding beauty concerned themselves less with establishing its validity and more with how it is perceived. Personal iconography grew to include brains and wheels. In a continuation of her puns, a 1993 still life is titled *Still Alive,* and another sculpture of the same year, *My Computer Has Wings,* celebrates her newfound tool for communication and design. There is also *Cool Dude* (1993), a tribute sculpture to Kursh, with his portrait and a torso-shaped armature filled with imagery of his favorite things. Once again Ruffner's work became more personal, a way to explore what happened and what has changed.

In 1993 two new series emerged, one in lampwork, the Balance Series, and one in collaboration with Kursh, Patterns of Thought. The second revealed yet another facet in Ruffner's art. Until this point, she had never done a collaboration that involved glass. Working with Kursh seemed a natural outgrowth of their time spent together during her recovery, and in addition, their individual work had lines of similarity. Before moving to New York to pursue painting, Kursh had been a sculptor in San Francisco. His mixed-media creations often carried humorous overtones, and in their own way projected a curiosity about things similar to Ruffner's. Talking about art is natural for Kursh and Ruffner, and Patterns of Thought developed when they both were artists in residence at Pilchuck. As Kursh explains, "Being together twenty-four hours a day when you're a couple and artists, there is that kind of unofficial collaboration. But Pilchuck was our first opportunity to really get together and make some work. We'd draw together, me finishing hers, she finishing mine. We didn't sit down and make a plan; it just happened." There, where artists are so often encouraged to mix blown glass with other media, it seemed natural to turn to the expertise of the artists in the hot shop and to utilize Kursh's skill with metal.

The first piece was a wire head filled with and spilling out a glitter of blown balls—grapefruit yellow with black dots, licorice black with *lattecino* stripes, lime green with orange swirls, champagne gold and raspberry wine with strawberry filigree. As the series progressed, the wire armatures became urns, goblets, and candy dishes larger than life, as though a Gulliver had set down his glass of bubbly among the Lilliputians. Like Ruffner's earliest work, they are about containment as well as loss, or excess when tipped—a goblet spilling champagne or a cornucopia overflowing. Though the works are not directly narrative, the series title, Patterns of Thought, pushes us to look beyond the lusciousness of the glass and the individual titles—*Eye Candy* (p. 102), *Ektachrome* (p. 103), *Sweet Thoughts* (all 1994)—with their sweet allusions to reverie and color.

The repetition that produces pattern is everywhere, on the glass, in the uniform size of the balls, and in the grids of the wire containers. Yet each ball is unique and a discrete part of a whole when held within the vessel. In their varied mix, they lend similarity to the containers without any two pieces ever being exactly the same. In them Ruffner sees

> a weaving of superficially disparate elements, creating resonance by their juxtaposition, placement, and balance. They seem to have many analogies to my life and brain. As a multitude of similar objects with very different surfaces, which are given another shape by the vessel they're in, they are a physical representation of thoughts—each similar though very different in content and expressed individually.

Because they are so immediately gorgeous, the balls also provide direct commentary on the relationship of glass to the decorative arts versus the fine arts. "In glass it's always said it's a danger to be too beautiful. We decided to discover if that were true and make the most beautiful thing we could." The issue of what is acceptable in art and craft thematically ties these pieces to Ruffner's lampwork and harkens back once again to Duchamp.

Yet to see the Patterns of Thought pieces as mostly Ruffner would be a mistake. They do not, despite their suggestiveness, depend in any way on narrative. They also possess a spareness and reserve that is Kursh's. Both artists agree that if either of them were doing this body of work alone, it would be very different. As Ruffner puts it: "It's a collaboration in the truest sense because if you look at his work and mine, you can see both of us in it. It's like a child that looks like the mother but smiles like the father."

Nonetheless, the collaboration raises some difficulties, concludes Ruffner, who likes her autonomy: "You can't get your way all of the time. Learning to compromise has been a big lesson for me." But if compromise can be seen as part of pragmatism, then it also extends into all her new work.

For instance, in the new lampwork, the Balance Series, the individual pieces are smaller than the massive ones done in the early 1990s, so that Ruffner can pick them up with her right hand and wheel them in her lap to a low workbench, where she can apply the less detailed color: "I need to be careful. My right hand is still not all that coordinated. I can carefully pour dye on the piece, have it wash over it—the Helen Frankenthaler approach!"

The Balance Series is also more reminiscent of the Beauties in frequently having a central active figure:

When I started this series, it was only about my own physical sense of balance, but it has extended out from there to other areas that need balance, like life and art, and relationships. Each piece usually has a solitary figure with an animal head or a Martian head performing various tricks. That is what I think you do in life: you do tricks by yourself. Often those who do the best tricks become famous. There's no implication of duplicity in that word. By trick I mean something that is powerful, mysterious, something that inspires a sense of wonder in others. In that sense, that is what art is, and what artists do. It's what I want to do.

In *Balance Series/The Original Checker Cab* (1994, p. 90), a piece reminiscent of the first Beauty *(Beauty Learning from the Past),* an acrobat in the Fool's traditional multicolored motley balances a fish and an urn on his head while riding atop a checkered dinosaur supported on three legs by a gem, an artist's palette, and a bone. "I wanted to indicate that he was supported by my experiences," explains Ruffner. In others from the Balance Series, foxes in black-and-white-striped shirts balance China teapots on one foot, or pair up to do cartwheels in the hedgerows. A black-and-white cat very like Ruffner's own pet, Studley, plays mirror games with a Martian or lifts barbells while zooming cross-country, one foot on an airplane, one in a lifeboat. This last piece, titled *My Cross-Country Relationship* (1995), illustrates for Ruffner the strength one gains in the difficult balancing act of long-distance love. The chicken also reappears once again on the move in *Balance Series/Another Way for the Chicken to Cross the Road* (1994, p. 93), this time on a wheeled conveyance that is a bone.

Because the works are smaller, singular, and more clearly personally narrative, the Balance Series has the feel of Ruffner's early story-pieces of the 1980s. Even though therapy and hard work have greatly improved Ruffner's speech and ability to use her body (in a letter to her mother in the summer of 1994 she related, "I walked two blocks today and didn't fall down or spit on anybody, so I count it a success"), she continues to struggle with learning to walk without assistance and to speak clearly without tiring. These concerns show up constantly in the imagery and titles that deal with locomotion and mental acuity: *The Martian Theory of Balance, Learning to Cat Paddle,* and *The Power of the Mind* (all 1995). The Balance Series is not so much a turning back as a continuation, an expression of her humor in the face of life's absurdities:

I'm real big on dealing with the hand you've been dealt. Nowadays I cannot manage those big pieces so easily. They are difficult for me to move around. They also don't seem symbolically as appropriate as they were at another time because right now what I'm dealing with in my life and my art is very focused. It's difficult, but that figure is managing. I have been dressing the figure similarly in every piece, in things I would like to wear. I can't find the clothes so I make them. The figure has an animal head or a space-alien head because I feel different from the rest of the human race and interested in more basic things, like an animal would be. This is the new alter ego. I think you should be able to change alter egos at will. You make them up, you can unmake them, too.

Like Ruffner herself, her inventions are getting where they need to go with true innovation, amusing us with their stunning tricks along the way.

In the spring of 1994, the two new series were brought together twice, once at Maurine Littleton Gallery, Washington, D.C., where the Balance Series was shown for the first time, and at the Bellevue Art Museum, Washington, in a show on painted glass curated by Seattle glass artist Dick Weiss. In the latter, the Patterns of Thought Series was expanded into an installation entitled *The Beauty Trap.* It featured three common types of traps—a wooden box propped on a stick, a suspended net (disguised as an outlandish chandelier decorated with gold fortune cookies and red lips among its baubles), and a hinged, steel maw with sharpened teeth—all using the opulence of the patterned blown glass for bait. Viewers could enter the huge traps if they dared. Though Ruffner and Kursh declared that the title alluded to the "trap" of making beautiful art, it was a natural extension to see it also as commentary on Western society's emphasis on personal beauty as a criterion for success in love and life.

Ruffner and Kursh intend to continue exploring these series at least through 1995. Patterns of Thought is already changing. Some of the containers have abandoned their classical roots and, like jazz musicians playing changes on a standard melody, developed free-form bends and irregularities. Some of the balls, finding the counterpoint, become containers themselves and hold evocative objects—hair, screws, pencils.

Another type of work, chandeliers, has slowly evolved into a series for Ruffner and may soon find a public venue as well. The first chandelier Ruffner made was a miniature, part of the set in a parody piece called *Phantom of the Igloo* (1988). Her designs for Vistosi in 1989, however, included a full-size, fully working blown chandelier replete with the Ruffner alphabet of hands, fish, dice, hearts, and snake, which curator Susanne Frantz convinced Ruffner to donate to the Corning Museum of Glass (p. 45).

Since then Ruffner has played with decorating found fixtures as well as created chandeliers out of various armatures left over from her installations. Ruffner notes, "When pieces sit in the studio, they are fair game for change." A 4-foot-long glass tornado, part of a piece from her installation *The Pursuit of Beauty*, first was sawed off its base to be hung in a corner as part of the installation at the Renwick. Then it came to hang in Ruffner's studio, where it was given metal arms to hold lights and several football-size glass "eggs" blown for Ruffner by Italian master Lino Tagliapietra on his visit to Pilchuck in 1994. "It's still in process," claims Ruffner, as are several others now being fabricated from scratch. "Pretty soon it will get so crowded in here I'll have to show them just to make space," she laughs.

In December 1995, Ruffner and Kursh will be making an installation for the Tacoma Art Museum's exhibition *Gardens of Delight*. Preliminary drawings have been sketched—on dinner napkins—suggesting three areas of "topiary." Patterns of Thought pieces will be shaped into such things as a Grecian figure, benches, a fountain. A number of Ruffner's lampwork sculptures—definitely not garden variety—will be interspersed on pedestals.

Ruffner is also working on designs for a possible large-scale project for an interior space for the Discovery Channel's offices as well as preparing a proposal for the Para-Olympics (a competition for athletes with physical disabilities), which will be held in Atlanta, Georgia, in 1996.

As did seeing Duchamp's *The Large Glass,* and experiencing her grandmother's death, the auto accident has provided Ruffner a demarcation line, substantially altering her work as it has altered her life. Its long-range effects remain to be seen. Art continues to be Ruffner's east and west, north and south, that which feeds her spiritually and ties her to the universal mind. She interprets everything through the lens of art, even adversity. Pragmatic, and used to solving problems in her work, she strives to reperceive her physical challenges, working with them as she would the limitations of the glass or the paint, tuning her viewpoint as she once tuned her eyes:

As I was on the floor exercising, and was thinking about what to add to my chandeliers, I was struck by the fact that I am always thinking about making things. I was in the hair salon yesterday, and I was thinking of something great to do with that hair they throw away. That voice, or whatever it is, is always there. I can see all these possibilities (in all that hair for example), and it's very, very exciting. So, yes, I do see everything through the lens of art. But I think, as I've said before, you don't "do" art—you "are" an artist, a seemingly small distinction, but one, I think, that is critical. It is no longer a choice with me. I think when I was younger, it wasn't as strong. But as with many things, the more you use it, the stronger it gets.

One of the things they tell you in brain-injury recovery is to practice self-awareness; if you want to teach the brain new/old tasks, it needs to be aware of the body and of sensation. This practice has made me even more aware of the creative process, from genesis to manifestation, and aware of that "alternative" way of perception that it engenders. I also think that since my primary information-getting sense—sight—has been so drastically compromised, it has forced my perception to be impacted by the other senses, and that has actually heightened my creativity because I'm letting in all those other possibilities and awarenesses.

With Ruffner the possibilities seem endless. They are also consistently life affirming. Before she could work, while she was recovering in New York that first year, she would get images for pieces and write them down or put them in the computer ("so I could read my writing, which is so bad!"), and she was struck by the fact that the pieces were so upbeat. She adds, "I realized that I still wanted to make celebratory work. It seemed like the accident was showing me that was what I should do, because if anybody had an excuse to be in a bad mood or to make nihilistic art, I did. But I didn't want to. So I guess I had always been on the right track."

The first week of January 1995, I walked into the quiet of Ruffner's studio. Her assistants Jeff Simmons and Julie Haack sat relaxed at the big workbench, painting striped shirts and diamond-patterned breeches on two new Balance Series figures. Wearing flowered tights and black, high-top Nikes with velcro straps, Ginny sat in her wheelchair at the low bench in front of the window, sunlight streaming in on her hair. She was painting a dancing jester, carefully filling in the background with a steady right hand. "Ginny walked the three blocks to the Italian restaurant yesterday without assistance," volunteered Julie. We all smiled.

What new facet Ruffner will reveal in her work is anybody's guess. The underlying philosophies, however, seem predictable. New work is bound to involve fanciful connection, even impudence, given Ruffner's sense of humor. It will continue to explore the connections between Ruffner's life as an artist and the great gestalt of science, society, and relationships, and any dark ironies will be balanced by celebration and joy. As Ruffner would say, "Why not?"

The Secrets of Eye Hand Coordination, 1993
Lampworked glass and mixed
media, 21 x 21 x 11 in.
Collection of Amy A. Olswang

**Architecture Utilizing
Bamboo, Clouds, and Ivy**, 1993
Lampworked glass and mixed
media, 22 x 9 x 9 in.

Another Pretty Face, 1993
Lampworked glass and mixed
media, 15 x 20 x 11 in.

**The Hemispheres of the Brain
Containing Pattern**, 1993
Lampworked glass and mixed
media, 9 x 18 x 10 in.

pages 86–87
Machan Oasis, 1993
William T. Machan Elementary
School, Phoenix, Arizona
Steel, concrete, and tile,
14 x 28 x 20 ft.

I like to think in all these big, unanswered questions.
As an artist, I can make up any answer I want,
and there is no reason why I can't be
theoretically correct.

why not? I thought I'd put some art in the space:

**What's Really in the Space
between Integers?**, 1993
Lampworked glass and mixed media, 23 x 18 x
10 in. Collection of Mr. and Mrs. Richard Waitzer

On the Wings of Geometry, 1994
Lampworked glass and mixed media,
22 x 26 x 12 in. Collection of the artist

Balance Series/The Original Checker Cab, 1994
Lampworked glass and mixed
media, 24 x 21 x 8 in. Collection
of Mr. and Mrs. J. Ira Harris

Ascension of Woman, 1994
Lampworked glass and mixed media,
30 x 48 x 18 in. (variable)

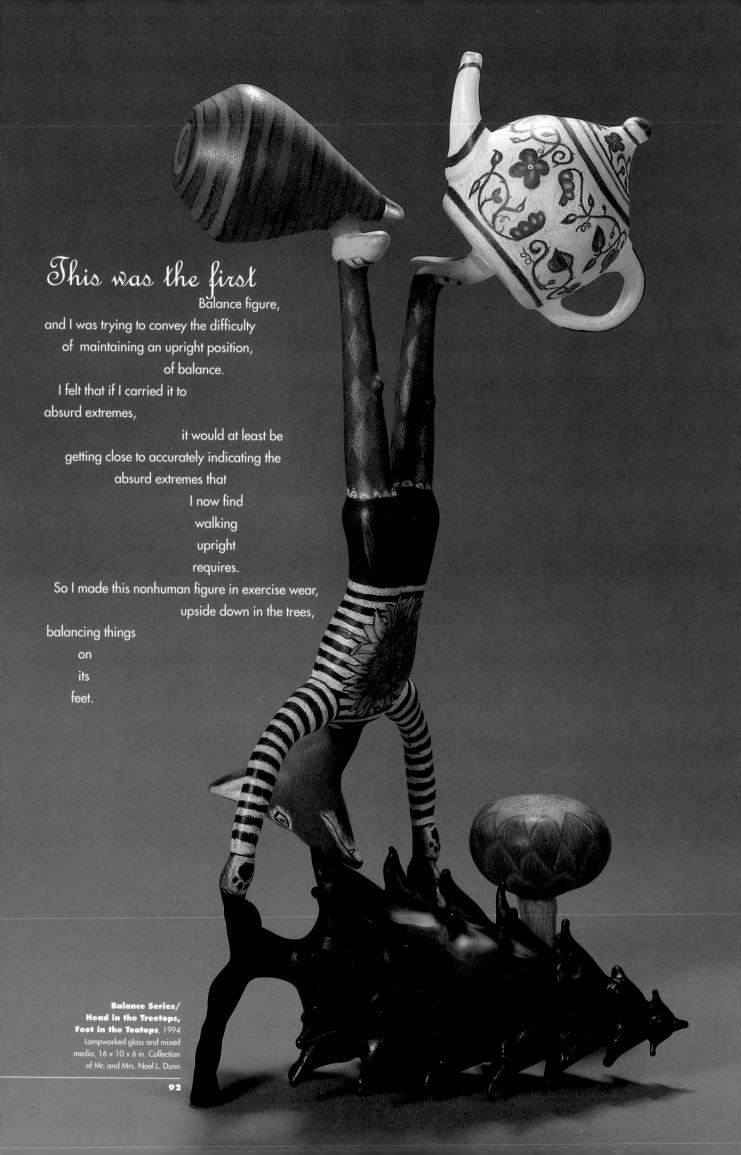

This was the first
Balance figure,
and I was trying to convey the difficulty
of maintaining an upright position,
of balance.
I felt that if I carried it to
absurd extremes,

it would at least be
getting close to accurately indicating the
absurd extremes that
I now find
walking
upright
requires.
So I made this nonhuman figure in exercise wear,
upside down in the trees,
balancing things
on
its
feet.

**Balance Series/
Head in the Treetops,
Feet in the Teatops**, 1994
Lampworked glass and mixed
media, 16 x 10 x 6 in. Collection
of Mr. and Mrs. Noel L. Dunn

This is the most recent in

my meditations

on the age-old chicken joke.

I wanted to make a Balance figure riding a chicken,
but then I thought,
"What can the chicken ride?"

I have always thought it was interesting that if you
mention the words

"chicken bone"

to people, the vast majority think of this shape,
which is of course only one of many bones in a chicken.

Given that perception, I thought it would make an
appropriate support,

and that the Balance figure should be attempting to
walk on

"chicken legs" (stilts).

**Balance Series/
Another Way for the Chicken
to Cross the Road**, 1994
Lampworked glass and mixed
media, 17 x 18 x 8 in. Collection
of Anne Gould Hauberg

**Balance Series/
A Different A Frame**, 1994
Lampworked glass and mixed media,
20 x 15 x 15 in. Collection of the artist

An Urn of Sea Shell Wine, 1994
Lampworked glass and mixed media,
16 ½ x 28 x 8 in. Collection of the artist

I wanted to make

a coiling, knotted form with protrusions,

one that on the whole would have a rather tight,

compact shape that folded back in on itself,

introspective, like a knotted rope.

When I saw the form in three dimensions, I knew that I wanted the surface to resemble a rope with a vine inside.

So in this case, the form, the surface, the concept, and the title all developed concurrently.

The piece suggested a question to which it was itself the answer.

I like that economy of conceptual means.

Why Ropes Coil, 1994
Lampworked glass and mixed
media, 5 ½ x 14 x 14 in.

The Rainbow in the Trout, 1994
Lampworked glass and mixed media,
14 ½ x 19 x 19 in. Collection of the artist

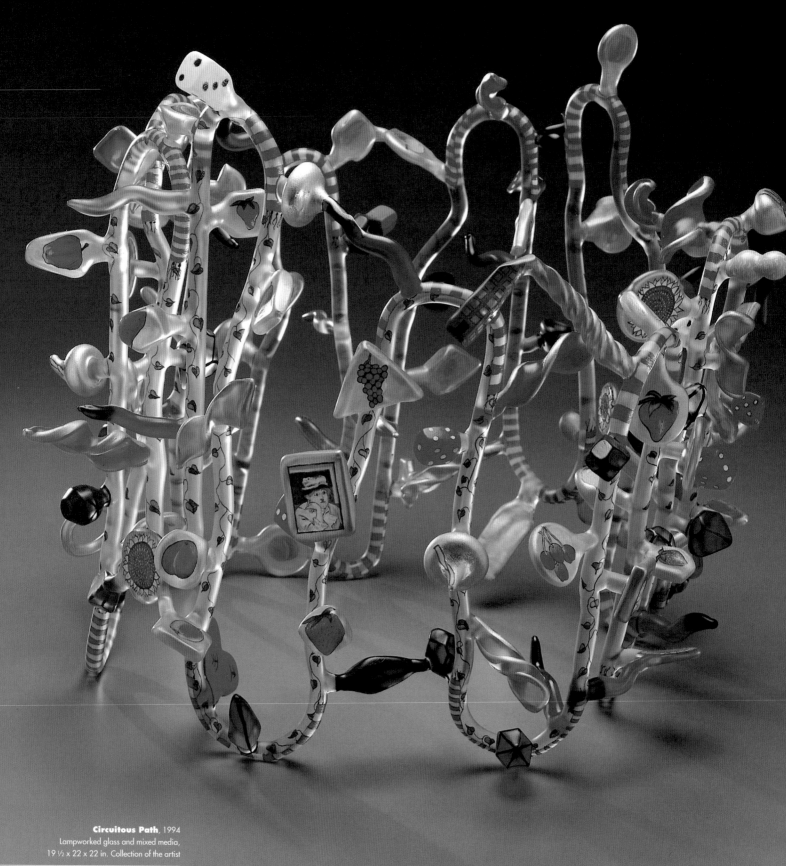

Circuitous Path, 1994
Lampworked glass and mixed media,
19 ½ x 22 x 22 in. Collection of the artist

It's All in How You View It, 1994
Lampworked glass and mixed
media, 15 x 7 ½ x 7 ½ in.

The conceptual intent of this installation was to point out that the oft-cited danger of glass
—that it's so beautiful—

is both its lure and its downfall, and to examine that claim:

i.e., what is so bad about beauty?

The bait balls were purposefully made to utilize as many of the exquisite glassmaking surface decoration techniques as possible and to accentuate their "glassiness" while they remained, ultimately,

a very simple form.

Many more interpretations can be drawn from this interest in the surface to the exclusion of the form itself.
The traps themselves offer other metaphors:

What prey is to be caught?

What is the lure of the balls—a desire for possession?

A desire for connection with the transcendent nature of true beauty?

Hunger?

As the one member of society charged with the creation of Beauty,

what is the artist's role in this hunt?

Ginny Ruffner and Steve Kursh
Installation view **The Beauty Trap**,
1994, Bellevue Art Museum, Washington
Glass, steel, trinkets, and mixed media,
8 x 8 x 8 ft. Collection of the artists

One of the things I have always liked about being an artist is that inventing things is part of the job.

Defining/manifesting unseen concepts in a visual format is one way to do that. The collaborative Patterns of Thought Series falls within that realm.

Collaboration, of necessity, originates cerebrally in that you must share ideas and communicate them through language. We consciously wanted to include an aspect of that

due to our recent, unexpected attention to brain functions. We also wanted to make the glass spheres as representative of the variety, multiplicity, and beauty of thought as we could.

These pieces continue to evolve as we experiment with both the container— the surface of the steel and the overall form where we're trying looser shapes

as well as more recognizable imagery—and the contents— adding evocative objects inside the balls to create allusions and layers of meaning. (We wanted these to be

B.Y.O.M., *Bring Your Own Meanings.*)

Ginny Ruffner and Steve Kursh
Patterns of Thought Series/
Eye Candy, 1994
Blown glass and steel, 16 x 16 in. diam.
Collection of the artists

Ginny Ruffner and Steve Kursh
**Patterns of Thought
Series/Ektachrome**, 1994
Blown glass and steel, 33 x 21 x 22 in.
Collection of the artists

Viewing the Seasons, 1994
Lampworked glass and mixed
media, 24 x 13 x 15 in.

Unusual Growth Patterns, 1994
Lampworked glass and mixed
media, 24 x 15 x 15 in.

I wanted to make a pair of the Balance figures

(which in this case symbolize collaboration)

wearing the same shirt but with different color emblems,

doing a very difficult stunt while supporting/hiding under a hedge.

The hedge turned out to be lots of individual leaves forming an overall shape—

which it is in real life—

but it still offered the desired suggestion of a

green, growing, vaguely sculptural form.

My personal definition of "hedging your bets" is

protecting yourself by diversifying your wagers—

a wise idea, especially if you are attempting complex, relatively untried maneuvers.

**Balance Series/
Hedging My Bets**, 1994
Lampworked glass and mixed
media, 15 x 16 x 5 in.

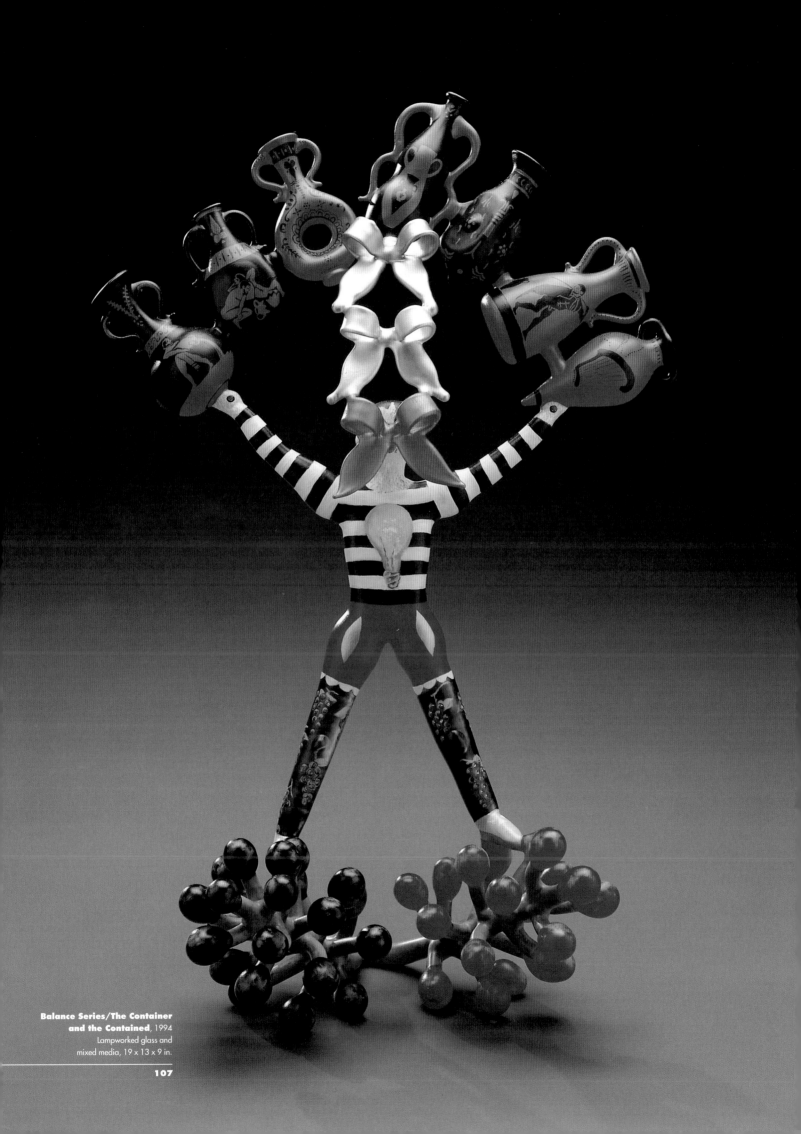

**Balance Series/The Container
and the Contained,** 1994
Lampworked glass and
mixed media, 19 x 13 x 9 in.

**Balance Series/
The Power of the Mind**, 1995
Lampworked glass and
mixed media, 7 x 9 x 6 in.

108

Balance Series/Classic, 1995
Lampworked glass and
mixed media, 16 x 10 x 10 in.

**Balance Series/Alternative
Locomotion**, 1995
Lampworked glass and
mixed media, 11 x 12 x 7 in.

**Balance Series/
Collaboration**, 1995
Lampworked glass and
mixed media, 5 x 16 x 9 in.

Notes

Unless otherwise noted, all quotations from Ginny Ruffner come from personal interviews conducted by the author between 1988 and 1995.

1. Sam Hunter and John Jacobus, *Modern Art: Painting, Sculpture, Architecture,* 3rd ed. (Englewood Cliffs, NJ, and New York: Prentice Hall and Harry Abrams, 1992), 169.

2. Paul Zelanski and Mary Pat Fisher, *The Art of Seeing,* 2nd ed. (Englewood Cliffs, NJ: Prentice Hall, 1991), 439.

3. Jessica Maxwell, "Ruffner," *New Work* (Summer 1988): 9.

4. Maxwell, "Ruffner," 11.

5. Tom Robbins, "Hair-Do Well," *Art & Antiques* (May 1987): 30.

6. Ginny Ruffner, "Speaking of Glass," *American Craft* (Oct./Nov. 1988): 32–35, 64.

7. Terry Barrett, *Criticizing Art: Understanding the Contemporary* (Mountain View, CA: Mayfield Publishing, 1994), 126.

8. Thomas Moore, *Care of the Soul: A Guide for Cultivating Depth and Sacredness in Everyday Life* (New York: HarperPerennial, 1994), 278.

Other sources of background information include Quentin Bell, *Bad Art* (Chicago: Chicago University Press, 1989); Randy Rosen, *Making Their Mark: Women Artists Move into the Mainstream, 1970–1985* (New York: Abbeville Press, 1989); and Paul Wood, et al., *Modernism in Dispute: Art since the Forties* (New Haven: Yale University Press, 1993).